Jewelry Making Handbook

By Iva L. Geisinger

CONTENTS

INTRODUCTION

Iva Geisinger is one of the country's most talented silver- and goldsmiths who has taught the subject to many students. Because of her great talent and originality of designs, she was chosen to write *Jewelry Maker's Handbook* as a series of for GEMS AND MINERALS Magazine where it was one of the most popular monthly features.

Iva wrote the series just as if she were personally teaching the reader how to make fine jewelry. To be sure that the illustrations were just right, she did her own photographs and drawings.

In this book you will find a wide variety of techniques, starting with simple projects and progressing right up to doing your own designing. And, you can get started without breaking the bank. By following these easy-to-understand instructions, you can open a new world of enjoyment and creation.

Part 1

Learning to make jewelry can be fun! It need not be difficult or expensive unless the participant chooses to make it so. As with most crafts and hobbies, the jeweler can surround himself with much expensive equipment or easily get by with a minimum. He can labor and fret, make a mountain of work, or he can relax and enjoy it.

The purpose of this *Handbook* is to make learning to create jewelry enjoyable right from the start. The beginner will be introduced to an exciting craft in simple, easy-to-follow steps.

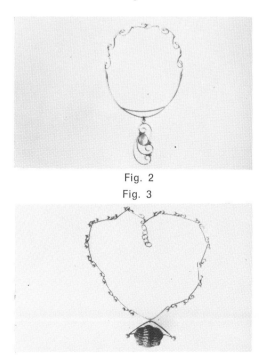

Fig. 1

Succeeding chapters will cover basic techniques of a variety of jewelry making procedures such as: soldering, sawing, smoothing, polishing, chasing, forging and forming. Also included will be the general application of basic tools. All of these are important steps if one wishes to graduate into a broad scope of intermediate and advanced hand-wrought jewelry making. Once a moderate skill in these fields is attained, there are endless combinations of materials with which to experiment to keep fine jewelry making an ever fresh and challenging experience.

Before learning how to make jewelry, it is well to know a little about the intended uses of particular pieces. These different functions may have a

Fig. 2

Fig. 3

Photo Data

Fig. 1 — Gold "basket" ring created by designer/craftsman, Richard D. Austin

Fig. 2 — Silver necklace by the author

Fig. 3 — Silver necklace with a trilobite as the center of interest

direct bearing on the design of a piece—whether it is to be lightweight, simple or ornate, etc. Primarily, jewelry is made to be worn as an enhancement to one's person. It can be utilitarian, as are hair combs, buckles or cuff links. Or, it may be an artful complement to a costume, such as a brooch, pendant or a pair of earrings.

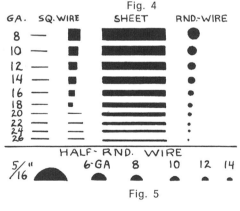

Materials

Jewelry can be made from many different materials. Some of the more commonly used include: a variety of metals, gemstones, beach pebbles, marine fossils, enamels, colorful seeds, plastics, leather and fur. Figure 4 shows a ring set with a beach pebble, the work of Eben Haskel, designer, craftsman.

This handbook will deal generally with metals and stones. Primarily it will be concerned with silverwork which is more suitable, economically, to experimentation than using gold.

Some of the metals used in making jewelry are: gold, silver, copper, brass, bronze, monel, iron, steel, aluminum, pewter and nickel silver. Gold, silver and other nonferrous metals (those that do not contain iron or steel) can be purchased in sheet and wire form in various thicknesses which in this country are measured by the Brown and Sharpe gauge system. The type jewelry you wish to make will determine the gauge of sheet or wire to be used.

Fig. 4

GA.	SQ.WIRE	SHEET	RND.-WIRE
8	—	■	●
10	—	■	●
12	—	■	●
14	—	■	●
16	—	■	●
18	—	▪	●
20	—	—	●
22	—	—	●
24	—	—	●
26	—	—	·

HALF- RND. WIRE

5/16"   6-GA   8   10   12   14

Fig. 5

Fig. 6

The gauge chart (Fig. 5) can be used as an economical substitute for a wire and sheet metal gauge like the one shown in Fig. 6. However, the gauge is more satisfactory. You can purchase gauges from the suppliers who handle jewelry making tools and materials (sources will be discussed later).

The next several paragraphs give a few facts about some of the more common jewelry metals.

Gold

Pure gold is the most malleable and ductile of all the metals and is too soft in its natural form to be practical. To make it harder, other metals are added to form an alloy. The most common gold alloys used in jewelry are: copper and gold (or silver, copper and gold) for yellow, and platinum or palladium and gold for white. Gold is measured on a *karat* system. Pure gold is known as 24 karat (24k) or 1.0000 *fine*; 10k contains .4167 fine gold; 14k has .5833 fine, is more malleable than 10k and is most commonly used in jewelry; 18k contains .7500 fine and is softer and more ductile than 14k. For jewelry, 18k gold is more suitably used in pieces not exposed to surface wear such as that to which finger rings are subjected.

Silver

The second most malleable metal, silver, is also too soft in its pure state, except as a base for enameling and in bezel wire. In its pure form this metal is known as fine silver. It is alloyed with copper for greater strength and durability. Sterling silver is the alloy most commonly used in good jewelry. It contains 925 parts fine silver and 75 parts copper, and is generally easier to work than karat gold.

Silver and gold complement each other nicely. Figure 7 shows a pendant made with wire and sheet of both these metals.

Fig. 7

Copper

Used most commonly as a base for enamel work, copper is, however, coming back into prominence for costume jewelry (Fig. 8). This metal takes good coloring effects by oxidation processes, but also oxidizes easily when exposed to air. It should be coated with a protective lacquer or acrylic, or brushed with melted beeswax if a polished surface is desired. Thin sheets make good patterns for jewelry designs because of the malleability; heavier gauge sheets provide good practice material for chasing. Copper can be purchased at many hobby and sheet metal shops.

Fig. 8

Brass

This is an alloy of copper and zinc and can also be purchased in sheet form. It is useful in inlay work (see picture) and as a practice material. Brass soon oxidizes without a protective coating.

METAL INLAY
SILVER, COPPER, BRASS
with:
NIELLO & PULVERIZED
TURQUOISE MIXED WITH
EPOXY.

Mohs' Scale of Hardness
1 — Talc
2 — Gypsum, alabaster
3 — Calcite, pearl
4 — Fluorite
5 — Apatite
6 — Feldspar
7 — Quartz
8 — Topaz
9 — Corundum (sapphire, ruby)
10 — Diamond

Fig. 9

Gemstones

Before selecting gemstones for a jewelry project, one should first be aware of the hardness and other characteristics. This is necessary in determining where the gem should be used according to its exposure to abrasion or abuse, and also to the care with which it should be handled. A book describing gemstones and their characteristics and properties is good background reading for the beginning jeweler. Take notes from one at your local library or purchase a good book on gem cutting and/or gemology.

There are two basic categories of gem cuts: 1. Cabochons which have domed tops and a wide varieties of shapes, such as ovals, rounds, hearts, rectangles, etc., and 2. Faceted stones, cut with a series of small flat planes, usually clear or translucent. Baroques (tumbled gems) also make attractive settings for abstract metal designs.

In addition to gemstones, materials such as exotic woods, ivory and bone can be used as striking contrasts to metals. They can be bezel set or inlayed. Figure 9 shows a bracelet set with osage orange and ebony wood—the work of Jim Agan, art metals instructor, Carmel, California.

Study and Reading Projects
From the library, rock shops and catalog suppliers there are various books available on the history of jewelry and related subjects that are worth-while reading. *The Autobiography of Benvenuto Cellini* is quite useful and interesting. Probably most of our readers are gem cutters; if not, books on gemology and gem cutting will furnish data that is useful for those who wish to purchase cut gems for their jewelry making projects.

Sources of Supply
Check with your local rock shops for silver and other metals, tools, supplies, gemstones, etc. Also, read the ads in rock hobby magazines. You will notice that some of the advertisers specialize in jewelry makers' needs. Some of the catalog suppliers stock quite extensive lines. In various parts of the country, there are several rock shops that give lessons in jewelry making. Exotic woods are available from: Craftsman Wood Service Co., 2729 South Mary Street, Chicago, Illinois 60608. A catalog is available from this firm.

In the next chapter the author will show several ways to set up a jewelry shop and discuss some of the equipment and tools.

Part 2 — The Work Area

Before making jewelry you will need to prepare an area in which to work. It can be an extra bedroom, any available corner in which to set up a table or, if you are fortunate, a shop. Here are a few ideas to help you plan your work area.

Any table with a drawer that will hold tools can be utilized (Fig. 10). It should have an overhanging top of about ¾- or 1-inch thickness on which to mount a table vise (available from rock shops and through jewelers' supply catalogs). Additional tools can be mounted on pegboard behind the table. Pliers and similar tools can be at your finger tips by forming a shallow U-shaped metal strip (or a piece of leather) and mounting it on one side of the bench.

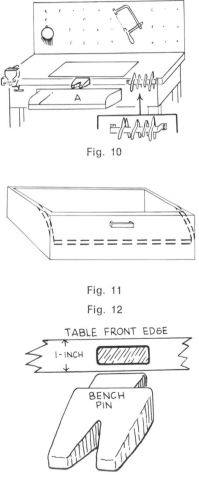

Fig. 10

Fig. 11

Fig. 12

Old desks, or the unfinished type, also make good work benches. Finish or refinish them as you see fit. A used furniture store may be an economical place to shop. Some metalcraft catalogs list jewelers' benches.

A common drawer can become a bench tray (Fig. 10A and Fig. 11) by sawing away a section of the front and sides. This tray can be pulled out to catch metal-filings.

For added durability and protection, ½" hard, fireproof material, such as mineral fiber sheet (an asbestos substitute available from some building supply or refractory firms), can be fitted and attached to the bench top. Or, a smaller sheet, about 11x14 or 16x20 inches can be substituted and used without permanent attachment.

From a rock shop or catalog supplier, purchase a hardwood bench pin—clasp-

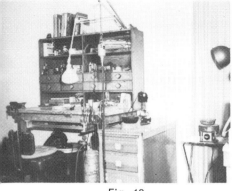

Fig. 13

Fig. 14

Fig. 15

Fig. 16

on, plug-in or screw-plate type, whichever your table will accommodate. Or, make one yourself. A bench pin is a standard accessory which is attached to the front edge of the work table. It is used to brace metalwork being sawed or filed. If purchased without the V front (the one in Fig. 12 has the V front), one can be sawed in by hand, filed and sanded smooth. Many jewelers prefer the V front for easier sawing.

Note: More complete data about tools, equipment and supplies will appear in Chapters 3 and 4.

A more elaborate working area (Fig. 13) includes a large work table with top-mounted drawers and cupboards, side cabinet, overhead light and a flexible shaft tool. An acetylene tank and torch is placed conveniently at hand. The torch is held secure to the front edge of the table by a spring clamp.

A rack to hold smaller fuel tanks can be attached and braced to the bench legs. Or, if a small hand torch unit, such as the Bernz-O-Matic propane tank, is used, it should be stored safely away when not in use.

Television trays (Fig. 14) can be used for extra table space. Their size makes them handy as portable units to move about wherever they may be needed.

Another point to consider is adequate ventilation. A hood with a vent fan, similar to those used over kitchen ranges, is a good feature to incorporate into your shop plans. It should be located over the working area to help whisk away polishing abrasives, fumes from melting solder and hot pickling solutions, and other air pollutants.

You can purchase a portable shop vacuum (Fig. 15) which can be moved about the area as needed. If neither of these methods is used, at least make sure there is good window ventilation.

In addition to good ventilation, a face mask (Fig. 16) should be used to help filter out polishing and grinding dusts.

JEWELRY MAKING — 6

It is advisable to have safety glasses (Fig. 16) handy for soldering, grinding, etc.

A swivel office chair can be a comfortable addition to your work area, but it should not be raised higher than the average chair. To avoid painful backaches, do not sit so that you must bend over your work to see it. Position yourself at a table level closer to your eyes (Fig. 17).

Fig. 17

The design area can be simply a space for pencils and a drawing tablet. An extension of a counter or a card table may be used — whatever your space and funds will permit.

Good lighting is a must. A combination of an overhead fluorescent fixture and a bright, closer, adjustable incandescent lamp works well. High intensity lamps (Fig. 18) are fine for close work, especially when the budget is limited.

Ample electric plugs should be handily available. Try to avoid the use of extension cords. Plug in only one or two electrical appliances at a time, or check with an electrician to make sure you have adequate circuits for several units. Everything electrical should be properly grounded.

Fig. 18

Fig. 19

As water is used frequently, it should be handy to the working area. If it is to be included in a shop plan, for safety, be sure it is partitioned away from any electrical appliances.

Small portable cabinets with sectioned drawers (Fig. 19) make good storage for such small items as findings and gemstones. They take up little space and can be set up in any convenient area.

On the following page is a diagram of a typical workshop area. Others contain less features and many have more. This is merely a plan to give the beginning jeweler ideas on which to base his own plans. Those who intend to do casting, silversmithing, gem cutting, plating or enameling may wish to include facilities for these as well. However, most beginners will undoubtedly start with a minimum amount of equipment and expand after they are more sure of their interest in the field of art metalwork and as they gain knowledge.

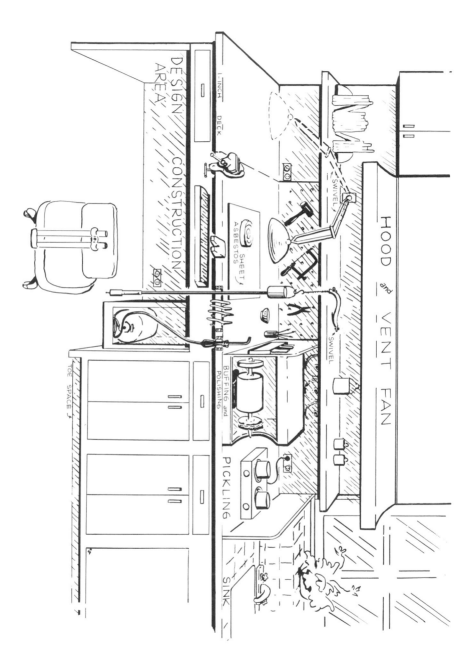

Part 3 — Tools and Equipment

Modern man has introduced many new and specialized tools and techniques for working with metals. However, jewelry is still fashioned by many of the same basic procedures used by early craftsmen. It is still constructed with solder or cast, scrolled, forged, pierced annealed, polished, colored, enameled, etc. Jewelers from many parts of the world still use many of the same ancient methods as their earlier counterparts, turning out pieces which compare in beauty and intricacy to those made with a multitude of modern tools.

The beginning jeweler, too, can start with comparatively few tools. He should choose them carefully, looking for good quality and multi-purpose use, when possible.

Here is a list of equipment which many jewelers find useful. Figure 22 shows those tools which the author considers necessary for beginning. Other important pieces of equipment are marked with an asterisk.

Table Vise — The vise shown in Fig. 20A does treble duty: 1. A small anvil is part of the body. 2. The undersides of the jaws are stepped to hold a solid ring mandrel (Fig. 20B). 3. The primary purpose of a vise is to hold work steady while it is sawed, filed or worked in some other way. It is used when it is difficult or awkward to work with a bench pin.

Bench Pin — See Chapter 2, *The Work Area*, Page 5.

Lead Sheet (Fig. 21) about ¼ inch thick and 12 inches square. Try plumbing supply shops for this item. It is mainly for forming, but can be used in some circumstances to keep metal steady while it is being stamped or worked in some other way. A lead sheet or block can be a temporary substitute for a dapping die.

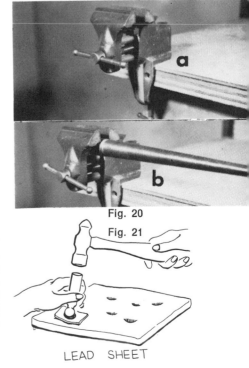

Fig. 20

Fig. 21

LEAD SHEET

1. *Rawhide Mallet*, 3½-ounce. Used to shape and hammer metal with a minimum of scarring and stretching.
2. *Ball Pein Hammer*, small, 4-ounce. For general work; custom hammers can be added later.
3. *Flat Hand File*, fine to medium cut, 8-inch length. General filing purposes.
4. *Jeweler's Shears or Snips*, 7-inch, straight blade. To cut thin sheets of metal and snippets of solder.
5. *Round Nose Pliers* (Long Nose), smooth jaws, 5½-inch length. For curving metals (such as wire scrollwork), forming links, etc.
6. *Chain Nose Pliers* (Long Nose), smooth jaws, 5 1/8-inch length. Can be used as a holding instrument when forming wire; to work with links; or, together with flat nose pliers, to straighten or open jump rings; etc.
7. *Wire Cutters* (end or side cutters). Quality cutters are recommended for best service in cutting various sizes of silver or gold wire.
8. *Tweezers*, 4- to 5-inch, general purpose. Used to pick up and arrange small items, such as solder snippets, jump rings, wire sections to be soldered, etc.
9. *Setting Burnisher*, 2-inch, curved blade. For pressing bezels against stones, etc.
10. *Steel Tracer or Scribe*, sharp point. To lay out designs on sheet metal.
11. *Ring Clamp*, double end. A wooden hand clamp with leather lined jaws that holds rings and other work for filing and stone setting.
12. *Jeweler's Saw Frame*, 5-inch depth, adjustable length. This size is a little awkward for the beginner, but it is more versatile in the long run. Select a variety of saw blades ranging in size from Nos. 0 or 1 (general work) to 4/0 (fine). This tool is used to saw sheet metals and wires of heavier gauge that cannot be easily cut with shears or wire cutters. A good rule of thumb for blade selection is: at least two saw teeth for the thickness of the metal being cut.
13. *Needle Files* — (a) round, (b) half round, (c) square, (d) knife, (e) barrette, (f) round edge joint. You can purchase a complete set which includes these shapes. A 4½- to 6¼-inch length, fine cut is recommended. For filing in small or hard-to-reach areas.

Not Shown

Tapered Ring Mandrel, solid steel, with graduated sizes. This handy tool is not mentioned in the minimum tool requirements, but is an almost indispensable piece of equipment for most jewelers. It can be used to form ring shanks, enlarge ring bands and to true resized ring shanks. Also, it is useful for forming other curved or circular pieces.

Bezel Mandrels. These come in various shapes — round, square, oval, etc. They are used to form bezels (the rims on some mountings which hold the gems), graduated links, etc.

Sources of supply — rock shops, catalog suppliers, advertisers in rock hobby publications.

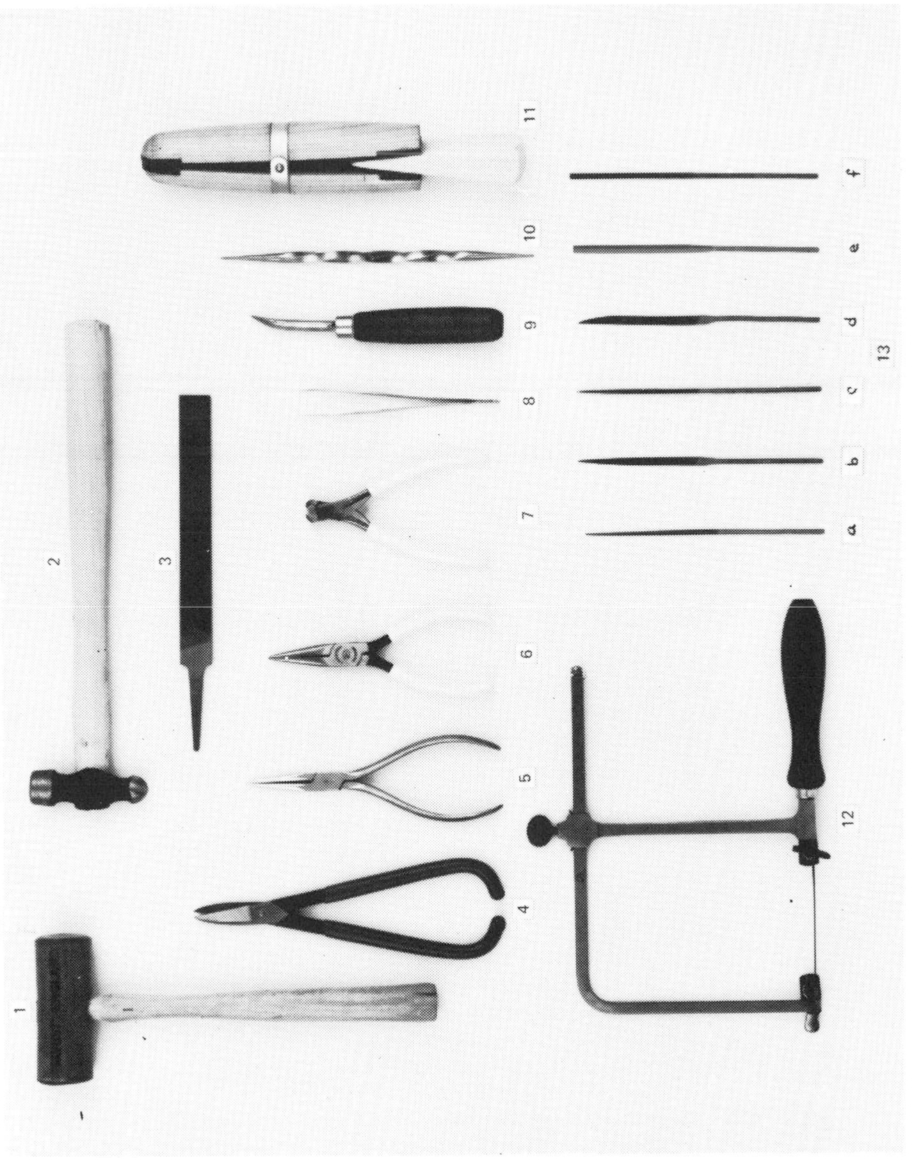

Fig. 22. Photo Courtesy of Southwest Smelting and Refining Co.

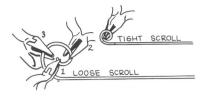

Fig. 23

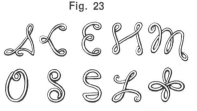

A FEW DESIGNS BASED ON LETTERS OF THE ALPHABET

Fig. 24

⟨SCROLL⟩	FROM	2½" - 16-GA. WIRE
⟨LINK⟩	FROM	1 ⅜" - 16-GA. WIRE
⟨CATCH⟩	FROM	1 ⅞" - 16-GA. WIRE

NECKLACE REQUIRES

17 SCROLL UNITS
16 LINKS
1 CATCH
16 BEADS (OPTIONAL)

Fig. 25

Fig. 26

ASSEMBLE BY LOOPING ENDS OF LINKS AROUND SCROLL WIRE

Exercise Project No. 1
A Scrollwork Necklace

This exercise is the first of a series to acquaint you with tools gradually. It will give you practice in filing and scrolling.

Tools and Materials

Round nose pliers (long nose), Fig. 22, No. 5

Chain nose pliers (long nose), Fig. 22, No. 6

Wire cutters, Fig. 22, No. 7

Flat hand file, Fig. 22, No. 3

16 gauge copper wire. Purchase at a hardware store.

Sanding paper or cloth, medium grit (No. 320 or 360, 2/0 or 0, depends on brand purchased)

16 beads, ¼-inch diameter (optional). Before purchasing beads, check for correct hole size by threading them on the wire.

For this practice exercise, buy a small roll of copper wire. It will stand up better to the twisting and re-twisting a beginning jeweler must do. Unless it is softened by annealing, sterling wire will become brittle under such treatment. Annealing will be covered in a subsequent chapter.

Scrolling (Fig. 23) — For small loops or circles, grasp one end of the wire with the tips of the round nose pliers and coil tightly. For larger scrolls, make looser coils, repositioning the pliers along the straight of the wire, and using the broader surface of the jaws of the pliers as the coil progresses. Masking tape, wrapped around the plier jaws will help prevent marring. Use the flat surfaces of chain nose pliers to straighten out unintentional bends.

To start, try a necklace of units with a simple S-scroll design. Later, create your own designs (Fig. 24). For the necklace, use wire cutters to snip the lengths called for in Fig. 25. File the ends flat, applying pressure on the strokes away from the body and raising the file on return strokes. With a small doubled-over square of medium grit sanding cloth or paper, remove **any sharp edges left by filing. (Good habits should be practiced from the beginning.) Prepare a few extra wires for trial and error. Assemble as shown in Fig. 26.**

Part 4 — Equipment, Tools and Supplies

The previous chapter carried a listing of basic tools for jewelry making. With those tools you can make simple items like the ones described in Exercise Project No. 1 (Part 3, Page 12). As you go on to more advanced work, buffing and soldering equipment and some other tools will be needed. The list below includes both low and higher priced equipment. Of course, the more expensive units deliver greater convenience and efficiency, but it is possible to do a good job with economy equipment. Asterisks note the important items.

*Buffing Equipment (Partial List)

Motorized Handpiece — The Dremel Moto-Tool (Fig. 27A) or a flexible shaft unit, like the Foredom (Fig. 27B), is an excellent investment because of the many uses to which it can be put. Numerous accessories can be purchased to saw, sand, grind, polish, drill, engrave, etc. The only drawback is that this type of unit is limited to fairly small pieces of jewelry. It is an excellent companion tool for a double spindle polisher (see below). On larger jewelry, use the handpiece for detail that could be dulled by bigger polishing wheels.

Emery Stick — for smoothing jewelry, removing scratches, etc., by hand.

Electric Belt Sander — special equipment.

Felt and Leather Buff Sticks — for hand polishing.

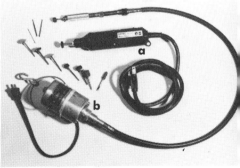

Fig. 27

Double Spindle Polishing Unit (Fig. 28), dust collector model recommended, rpm speed around 3450. This machine takes different accessories for grinding, polishing, buffing inside rings, etc. It's good for all larger jewelry and many small items. A felt wheel is a good extra accessory for working flat surfaces and sharp edges. For general buffing, 3- to 5-inch muslin and cotton flannel wheels are advised. Suggested accessories for beginners — 4-inch coarse muslin buff for use with tripoli compound, 4-inch fine muslin buff for yellow or white

Fig. 28. Photo courtesy Southwest Smelting and Refining Company

Fig. 29. Photo courtesy Southwest Smelting and Refining Company

Fig. 30

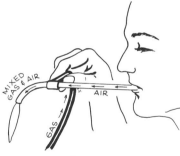

Fig. 31

Fig. 32

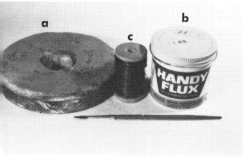

rouge, 5-inch cotton flannel or chamois buff for red rouge.

Soldering Equipment

Here are several types to consider. BE SURE to follow manufacturer's or dealer's instructions for safe use.

Acetylene Tank and Torch (Fig. 29) — favored by the author.

Oxygen Tank Units — Natural gas or acetylene can be used with an oxygen unit. Either combination will give a hotter flame (necessary when working platinum) than acetylene alone. Not recommended for the beginner.

Propane Tank and Torch Unit (Fig. 30) — self-contained, inexpensive and simple to operate. Has quite a hand bulk; be very careful not to drop it.

Blow Pipe (Fig. 31)—This inexpensive means of soldering has been used for many years. Heat can be supplied by either natural gas or an alcohol burner. Some practice is necessary in order to master the technique of maintaining an air supply in the cheeks while breathing through the nose and blowing through the mouth. Using the above fuels, however, limits the size of jewelry work. Obtain further operation and fuel information from a dealer.

Soldering Coil of Asbestos Substitute (Fig. 32A) — a base for general soldering. We urge you *not* to use true asbestos because it can be very hazardous to your health.

Wire Soldering Frame — A box or frame of wire which allows heat to be applied to the underside of a piece being soldered. In use, it is placed atop an asbestos *substitute* coil, charcoal block or pumice soldering pan.

Soldering Flux (Fig. 32B)—For coating joints to be soldered to promote solder flow and prevent excess oxidation (more details in a subsequent chapter). A paste, such as Handy Flux, is highly recommended for beginners.

Charcoal Block — For shot making and general soldering.

Iron Binding Wire (Fig. 32C) — Holds pieces together for soldering.

Striker — A handy gadget for lighting a torch.

Anvil (small) — For forging small work and miscellaneous uses.

Borax Slate — Used to mix a borax and water paste flux (a substitute for commercially bottled flux) and for holding solder snippets.

Chasing Tools — For chasing and repousse work. Used with a pitch bowl, hardwood block or lead sheet. These tools are made in assorted end shapes. Suggested for beginners: medium-small, straight lining tool; and a medium-curved stamping tool.

Copper Tongs — To retrieve metals from the pickling bath.

Dapping Die Block, steel — For use with dapping punches.

Dapping Punches — Used to make beads, form thin sheet metal into half spheres, cupping.

Electric Hot Plate with heat control — To heat pickling solutions, such as Sparex, in a copper pan.

Pickling Compound — Sparex No. 2 recommended for beginners instead of more hazardous acids. To clean oxidation (or fire scale) from gold and silver. Mix with water according to manufacturer's directions.

Flat Nose Pliers — Many holding and forming applications.

Gravers — Come in various end shapes for different purposes. Used generally to remove or displace metal by hand, i.e. design engravings, bead setting small stones (bringing up a narrow strip of metal next to a stone, then using a beading tool and chasing hammer to cap it over the edge of the gem), florentine finish (using line gravers to create a variety of fine finishes), removal of excess solder from hard-to-reach areas.

Half Round File — Used when it is necessary to file inside ring bands or other curved areas.

Hand Drill, chuck capacity 0 to ½ inch — for piercing sheet metal in order to insert a saw blade for cutout designs, and for general drilling. (Or use drills or cutters in a motorized handpiece.)

Pitch Bowl — A base for chasing and repousse work.

Planishing Hammer — To forge metals.

Set of Ring Sizers — Fit on fingers to determine ring sizes.

Stone Pusher — For pushing bezels against gemstones.

Stone Setting Burs — Used in the chuck of a motorized handpiece when setting round faceted gems.

Stone Setting Pliers — A specialty item. For setting or tightening prongs over stones.

Miscellaneous Supplies

Beeswax — For lubricating saw blades before cutting metal.

Liver of Sulphur (or a commercially bottled coloring solution) — To be used, generally with heat, for coloring (oxidizing) sterling silver and some alloyed gold.

*Metal Sheet, Gold or *Silver* — Order the gauge desired (refer to gauge chart, Page 2, Chapter 1).

Sanding Sheets — Waterproof silicon carbide cloth or paper, emery cloth or emery paper — coarse to fine grits. For removing surface abrasions by hand.

Solder, Gold — Purchase for the particular karat to be soldered and by approximate melting points. Examples:

          10K, yellow, easy (1340°F melting point)

          14K, yellow, easy (1310°F melting point)

          14K, yellow, hard (1463°F melting point)

Solder, Silver — Purchase all three listed:

          Easy (1325°F melting point)

          Medium (1390°F melting point)

          Hard (1425°F to 1475°F melting point)

Note: Use only silver solders when making silver jewelry, except in special instances. Details in a subsequent chapter on soldering.

Wire, Gold or *Silver* — Shapes are round, square, bezel, half round, etc. Order according to gauge and shape desired (refer to gauge chart, Page 2, Chapter 1).

Many other tools and supplies could be used, but the beginner can get along very well with a few chosen from those already listed. Send for jeweler's supply catalogs for a more complete listing.

Care of Tools

Drills and Cutters — Coat with oil frequently. Rust remover with protective agents can be purchased in aerosol spray containers. Keep cutters, drills, points, etc., handy in a styrofoam base or a drilled hardwood block (Fig. 33).

Gravers — A sharp graver is necessary at all times, so sharpen often. Graver sharpeners that will automatically preserve the angle of the cutting edge are available, or bench stones can be used for hand sharpening; both require an oil lubricant. Care should be taken to maintain the angle if a bench stone is used. If engraving is to become a major interest, a book on techniques should be studied, as well as basic jewelry making.

Pliers (and other iron tools) — When not in use, coat with oil frequently to minimize rust damage.

Files — Keep readily available in separate holders, i.e. box lids, wall racks (Fig. 34), etc. Keep dry to avoid rust damage.

In the next chapter is a project, making a pierced pendant. It will give you experience in using drills, a jeweler's saw, files and pliers.

HARDWOOD DRILL & CUTTER HOLDER

Fig. 33

Fig. 34

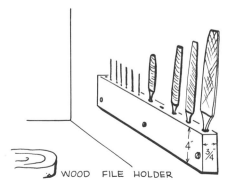

WOOD FILE HOLDER

Part 5 — Making a Pierced Pendant

In chapters 3 and 4, you were introduced to various tools, equipment and supplies. Now, here is Exercise Project No. 2 which will give you experience in using some of these items. Refer to the previous two chapters for descriptions. The techniques you will learn in this project are: 1. Threading and using a jeweler's saw, 2. Piercing, 3. Emery finishing (sanding).

Tools
Drilling equipment — hand drill or a motorized handpiece with a small round cutting bur
Needle files — See Part 3, Fig. 22, No. 13
Jeweler's saw frame and blades (Fig. 22, No. 12)
Flat hand file (Fig. 22, No. 3)
Round nose pliers (Fig. 22, No. 5)
Steel tracer or scribe (Fig. 22, No. 10)
Work bench or table, bench pin, sanding sheets and beeswax

Materials
20 gauge sheet metal — silver, brass or copper
16 gauge round wire, about 1-1½ inches for bail

Insertion of Saw Blade
Choose a blade which has at least two teeth for the thickness (gauge) of metal to be cut. Turn the saw frame so that the throat (blade side) is up. Loosen the bottom screw (see Fig. 35) and, with the teeth pointing toward the handle, insert the end of the blade. Tighten the bottom screw. Loosen the back screw and adjust the length of the frame so that the loose end of the blade is even with the inside edge of the top of the frame throat. Tighten the back screw. Loosen the top screw, brace the handle against your body, the top of the frame against a table edge, and push against the handle until the top end of the blade can be inserted well inside the clamp. Tighten the top screw while

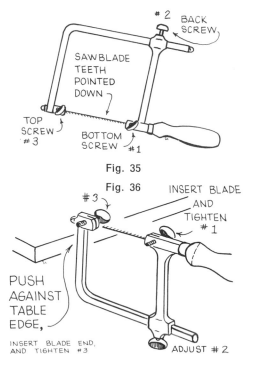

2 BACK SCREW

SAW BLADE TEETH POINTED DOWN

TOP SCREW # 3

BOTTOM SCREW #1

Fig. 35

Fig. 36

3

INSERT BLADE AND TIGHTEN # 1

PUSH AGAINST TABLE EDGE,

INSERT BLADE END, AND TIGHTEN # 3

ADJUST # 2

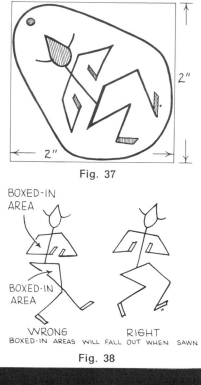

Fig. 37

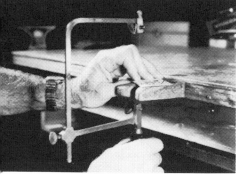

BOXED-IN AREA

BOXED-IN AREA

WRONG   RIGHT
BOXED-IN AREAS WILL FALL OUT WHEN SAWN

Fig. 38

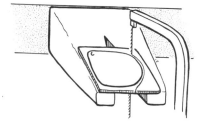

Fig. 39

Fig. 40

LEAVE A NARROW MARGIN AROUND PENDANT LINES FOR FILING SMOOTH.

still pushing. The blade should be taut, having a high-sounding *ping* when plucked with the fingernails. See Fig. 36.

The Project

With a soft-leaded pencil, draw the outline of the pendant and a design on a two-inch square of sheet metal. Use the design shown in Fig. 37 or one of your own. Incorporate thin, saw-blade-width lines, open areas, sharp corners and rounded curves; this will give good practice for several techniques of using a jeweler's saw. Do not box in any part of the design or it will fall out when cut with the saw (see Fig. 38).

Trace *lightly* over the design with a scribe. Pencil marks can be erased or become smudged; scribed lines are semi-permanent because they are scratched into the surface of the metal. In case of error, shallow scribe marks can be sanded away when the piece is being finished.

For smoother action, lubricate the saw blade by drawing it across a block of beeswax — only once. Too much wax will clog the blade so that it will not cut effectively.

Brace the square of metal on top of the bench pin, using the left hand, if you are right-handed (Fig. 39). Saw around the outline, leaving a narrow margin for filing (Fig. 40). The saw should be held straight up and down, with no tilt forward, backward or to either side. A tilted saw can bind and break at curves. Start with a down stroke, using little force, and cut with the full length of the blade for straight lines or large curves.

If there is difficulty in getting started: (1) try positioning the metal a bit back of the front of the bench pin so that the saw cuts a little of the bench pin wood before cutting into the metal. (2) Check to see if your blade is fine enough. (3) Try more wax lubricant (copper requires more than silver).

Don't make hard work out of sawing.

Relax, don't rush and don't force, or you'll find yourself breaking saw blades needlessly.

Pierce a small hole in the largest design area by drilling with a motorized handpiece, hand drill or a hammer and small nail. The metal sheet should be placed on a hardwood block (see Fig. 41). Drills or burs should be only large enough to accommodate the saw blade. To keep the drill from slipping, an indentation can first be made with a hammer and nail or center punch.

Loosen the top end of the saw blade and insert it through the hole from the underside; re-tighten the screw that holds the blade (Fig. 42). Saw out the design, leaving a narrow margin outside the lines for filing (except for saw-width cuts). Be careful to saw evenly on the blade-width cuts, for it would be extremely hard to refine these edges.

Small circles or sharp curves require shorter strokes than straight lines. At sharp corners, stop all forward movement and saw up and down, while slowly turning the blade, until the corner is completed, then continue with normal strokes.

After all sawing has been completed, smooth the larger cutout areas with needle files. Remember, to apply pressure on the forward strokes. The half round file can be used for inside curves, the flat side of the half round for straight edges or small outside curves, the knife edge or barrette for sharp inside angles, the round file for small circles or sharp inside curves. While stroking up and down, also keep the file progressing forward along the edge to produce a smoother finish (Fig. 43).

Pierce a small hole near the top of the pendant from which to hang a bail. Smooth the hole with a round needle file.

File the outside edges of the pendant smooth to the scribed lines with the flat hand file (Fig. 44). For better control, always use as large a file as possible.

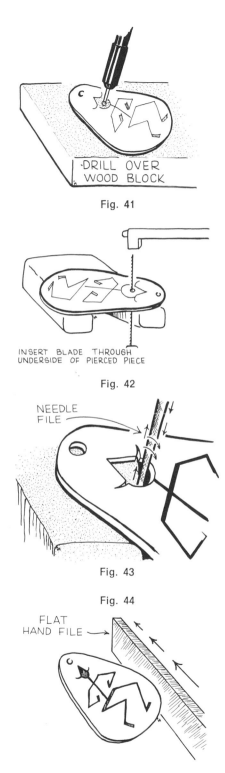

DRILL OVER WOOD BLOCK

Fig. 41

INSERT BLADE THROUGH UNDERSIDE OF PIERCED PIECE

Fig. 42

NEEDLE FILE

Fig. 43

Fig. 44

FLAT HAND FILE

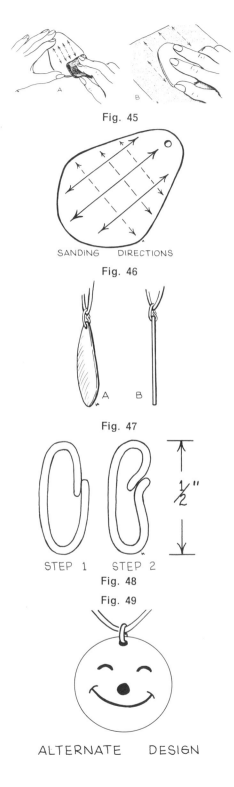

Fig. 45

SANDING DIRECTIONS

Fig. 46

Fig. 47

STEP 1 STEP 2

Fig. 48

Fig. 49

ALTERNATE DESIGN

Finishing

Remove scratches and other abrasions with medium grit sanding cloth or paper. One method is to double about 2 square inches of cloth or paper, as shown in Fig. 45A, and sand the metal surface. Doubling and using small amounts of abrasive material gives the jeweler better control.

Another method used for perfectly flat surfaces, such as this pendant, is to hold the metal in the fingers and move it across a large single layer of sanding cloth or paper (Fig. 45B). This produces a more even finish. With either method, don't be afraid to apply pressure.

Sand in one direction only, until all scratches disappear, then abrade at right angles to the first direction (Fig. 46). This will show up any hidden surface defects. Change to a medium fine grit paper or cloth and repeat the process. Repeat again with fine (500 or 600 grit, if using silicon carbide paper), ending with the sanding direction from the bottom of the pendant to the top. This will leave a fine brushed finish.

As you progress with your lessons, you may wish to cup your pendant somewhat with chasing tools (Fig. 47A). A rounded or shaped piece usually has more appeal and character than a perfectly flat one (Fig. 47B).

A simple wire bail can be made by using round nose pliers to bend 16 gauge wire into a long narrow oval (Fig. 48, Step 1), sanding the wire ends smooth and shaping as shown in Fig. 48, Step 2. The ends should overlap slightly, their inside surface touching together. Exercise No. 1, on scrolling, should help on this step. The pendant can now be hung on a cord or necklace chain.

As you progress, ideas for designs will probably present themselves. Perhaps you would like to make a Happy Face like the one shown in Fig. 49.

Part 6 — Introduction to Heating And Soldering Techniques

In making jewelry, we use torches for: 1. uniting two or more pieces of metal with hard solder; 2. melting metal for castings or small beads (shot), see Fig. 50; 3. heating metal in preparation for coloring — darkening, popularly known as oxidizing, with liver of sulphur or other commercial solutions; 4. annealing to restore the metal's malleability and ductile qualities; 5. hardening and tempering handmade steel chasing tools; 6. qualified enamel work, though a kiln is usually more desirable; 7. other purposes.

Possibly the most important phase of learning jewelry construction is that of correct soldering techniques. Because so much depends on the quality of a soldering operation, it is wise to practice at length to perfect the process.

A correct soldering flame can be recognized by sound and color. Jewelers should be able to distinguish the difference between a *reducing flame* and an *oxidizing flame* (see Fig. 51). An oxidizing flame is one which contains an excess amount of oxygen, and a reducing flame contains a minimum amount of oxygen. A loud hissing sound indicates a poor mixture of oxygen and gas; a change is needed. When working with gold or silver, more of a reducing type of flame should be used to prevent excessive oxidation which can prevent good solder flow.

Torches and Flame Zones
(Also see Part 4, Page 14)

Combination units, such as oxygen/gas torches allow oxygen adjustments. Because of the higher flame temperature, it is easier to overheat or melt delicate, handwrought jewelry. If the beginner insists on starting with this type of unit, the author recommends that he receive operating instructions from a dealer or jewelry teacher.

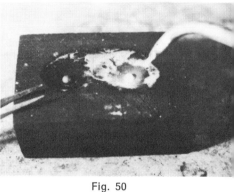

Fig. 50

Fig. 51

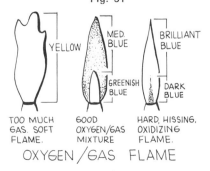

YELLOW	MED. BLUE	BRILLIANT BLUE
	GREENISH BLUE	DARK BLUE
TOO MUCH GAS. SOFT FLAME.	GOOD OXYGEN/GAS MIXTURE	HARD, HISSING, OXIDIZING FLAME.

OXYGEN/GAS FLAME

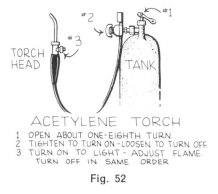

ACETYLENE TORCH

1 OPEN ABOUT ONE-EIGHTH TURN.
2 TIGHTEN TO TURN ON - LOOSEN TO TURN OFF.
3 TURN ON TO LIGHT - ADJUST FLAME.
  TURN OFF IN SAME ORDER

Fig. 52

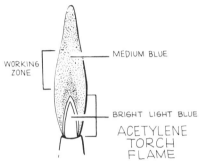

ACETYLENE
TORCH
FLAME

Fig. 53

Fig. 54

Fig. 55

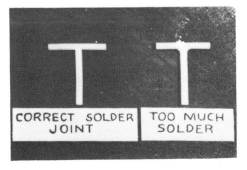

A self-contained acetylene torch, such as the Prest-O-Lite, has no special adjustment for oxygen because the gas mixes with air at the tip of the torch head (Fig. 52). Avoid a loud, hissing sound by regulating the torch head valve and valve No. 2 as shown in Fig. 53. Change to a larger tip if a larger flame is needed. Work fairly close to, but outside, the tip of the brilliant light blue zone of the correctly adjusted flame. Acetylene torch tips can be purchased in graduated sizes. Numbers 1, 2 and 3 are recommended for most jewelry work, the smallest being No. 1. Reserve No. 3 for larger pieces — about 4 square inches or more.

Propane and butane cannister torches (the self-contained units with disposable cylinders) are simple to operate. Some give about 15 hours burning time.

About Solder

Silver solder can be purchased in *hard, medium* and *easy*. These designations refer to melting points, hard having the highest and taking longer to melt than medium or easy. Beginners might be wise to use medium and easy for practice until they learn to control the torch and solder flow.

Solders are available in flat sheets, clipped chunks, wire and ribbon forms. Sheet solder is snipped into small squares. To do this, first make a series of closely spaced cuts into one end of the sheet, then cut across the first cuts (Fig. 54). These snippets should be tiny — 1/64th to 1/16th inch square depending on the size of the work. When applying solder, use only enough to produce a smooth joint; too much will create an ugly, bulky joint (see Fig. 55). It takes practice and experimentation to determine how much solder to use.

SOLDERING STEPS
Step 1
Prepare the Work For Soldering
A. Shape the joints to fit perfectly
B. Soldering bases. Place the work on a soldering base — asbestos

substitute coil, charcoal block or magnesia block. Use steel wire clamps or steel household or "bank" pins to hold the joining surfaces firmly in place and tightly together (Fig. 56). The use of iron binding wire will be discussed in Part 7.

C. Fluxing. Carefully apply a flux paste to the joint with a small pointed brush (Fig. 57). In doing this, avoid picking up foreign matter, such as magnesia or charcoal. The joint must be clean or the solder will not flow.

Fig. 56

D. Solder. Use the correct amount and kind of solder, placed properly (Fig. 58). The tip of the flux brush, dampened with flux, will not only aid in placing the solder, but will flux it at the same time. (Soldering Step 1, A, B, C and D, will be covered further in Part 7).

Fig. 57

Step 2
Applying the Torch

A. Put on your safety glasses. Light and adjust the torch flame. Keep the torch head pointed away from you when lighting; make sure no combustibles are in the flame area.

B. Dry the flux by circling the flame slowly around the work, without actually touching it. Heating the metal too quickly will cause the flux to bubble or foam, which in turn may move solder snippets out of correct positions.

C. As soon as the flux is dry, direct the torch flame to the work, moving more or less in a figure 8 pattern (Fig. 59) over the whole piece until the solder becomes fluid. The liquid appearance of the solder at joining seams is probably the best way to determine when the solder flows. Another indication is when a top piece drops down, such as a finding on a pin back or when pieces are layered.

D. Use tweezers to transfer the hot metal to cold water in a pyrex bowl so that the joints can be safely examined.

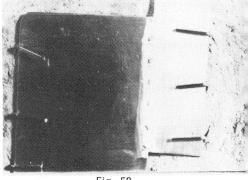

Fig. 58

Fig. 59

FLAME PATTERN

Note: Do not prolong the heating step. This will cause an excess of copper oxides to come to the surface (oxidation), which will be difficult to remove. Generally, the whole, piece should be heated as quickly as possible for a correct soldering operation. Concentration of heat in one spot may cause oxidation, pitting or melting of parts. Withdraw the torch as soon as the solder flows because each additional second will compound heat damage.

Practice Project No. 3

This exercise will give you experience in filing to fit, fluxing and wire-to-wire soldering.

USE ROUND NEEDLE FILE
TO SHAPE END TO FIT.

SOLDER
PLACEMENT

Fig. 60

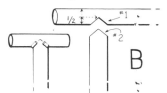

1 - USE SQUARE FILE TO INDENT.
2 - SHAPE TO FIT "∧" WITH
FLAT HAND FILE

Fig. 61

Fig. 62

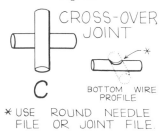

CROSS-OVER
JOINT

BOTTOM WIRE
PROFILE

✻ USE ROUND NEEDLE
FILE OR JOINT FILE.

Tools and Supplies

Torch and soldering supplies (see pages 14 and 16)
Jeweler's shears or snips (Fig. 22, No. 4)
Tweezers (Fig. 22, No. 8)
Flat hand file
Needle files
Wire cutters
14 or 16 gauge round sterling wire.

Because solder joints must fit together closely in order for the solder to flow properly, often one or both of the joining areas must be shaped. Practice making the joints shown in Figs. 60, 61 and 62 until you can do them easily. Use ½- to ¾-inch lengths of sterling wire.

Exercise A (Fig. 60)

1. Flatten the joining end of a wire with a hand file.

2. With a round needle file, make a curved depression in the flattened end. This depression should fit the surface of the joining wire (see illustration).

3. Remove the rough bur (curled edge created by the file) with a flat needle file. Very little pressure is needed. Burs make irregular joints.

4. Using small tweezers, fit the joining pieces in place on a level soldering base (see 1B, page 22).

5. Flux the joining areas with a small brush.

6. With the tip of the brush, apply 2 tiny snippets of medium solder (about 1/32-inch squares), one at the top of each side of the joint. Continue by following Soldering Step 2, A, B, C and D (pages 23 and 24).

Exercises B and C (Figs. 61 and 62) — Follow the instructions in the illustrations, applying the techniques you have already learned. More heating and soldering techniques will be covered in Parts 7 and 8.

Part 7 — Heating and Soldering

Now that you have been introduced to the materials and basic soldering techniques, it would be well to learn more about them. Silver solder is made mainly from silver, and gold solder primarily from gold. Each has small additions of other metals to form alloys with lower melting points than the basic metals. These are called hard solders (melting points above 1100°F) and should be used when soldering precious metals, except under special circumstances. An exception, for example, is when it may be necessary to use soft or low temperature solder to avoid melting a very small finding. Otherwise, lead-based or soft solders should be avoided when working with precious metals. They quickly eat into gold or silver under high temperatures, causing unsightly pitting and also lower the overall karat or sterling balances of these metals.

As noted in the previous section, solder can be purchased in flat sheets, clipped chunks, wire and ribbon forms. Each can be used practically, depending on the type of join. Sheet solders are probably best for general use. They should be given easy identification (Fig. 63) by scribing, on the surfaces, the initial of each one's particular hardness, i.e. H (hard), M (medium) or E (easy). Refer to Fig. 54 (previous chapter) for the method of cutting a sheet into snippets.

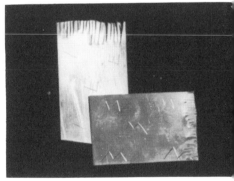

Fig. 63

Fig. 64

Keep snipped solders in separate small vials or jars with lids (Fig. 64). Label each container according to the kind of solder and its hardness.

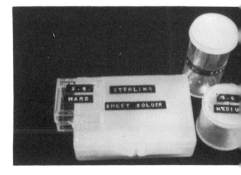

MORE ABOUT SOLDERING STEPS

(Also See Chapter 6)

Step 1

Prepare the Work for Soldering

A. Shaping Joints. Joints can be shaped for a close fit by filing and sanding. There are different kinds of joints, each falling into a particular category

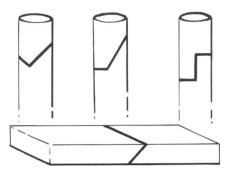

Fig. 65

Fig. 66

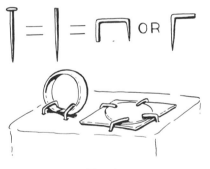

Fig. 67

Fig. 68

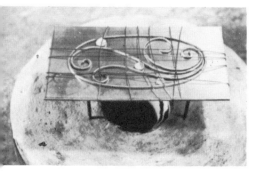

(to be described in Chapter 8). In the wire-to-wire type, where the wire ends meet in a "butt" joint, or where the end of one wire meets the side of another, greater strength can be had by first forming a bevel or "V." This type of joint (Fig. 65) may be desirable for stress areas or for mending a place where a joint with greater strength than an ordinary butt type is needed, such as a broken prong.

B. *Soldering Bases.* It is possible to get by with a charcoal block, only, for a soldering base. One side can be used as a flat surface and the other can be scraped until a hollow is formed where small pieces of metal can be melted to form solid, round beads (shot).

Other good bases are asbestos substitute coils, for flat work, and softer magnesia blocks for work where joints will fit together better when one or both parts are partially buried (Fig. 66)

C. *Bracing.* Use whichever means of bracing that will hold the particular joints together. It takes only a moment to cut off the head of a steel household or bank pin and shape it into a holder with chain nose and flat nose pliers. Two holders, pinned over the bottom of a round, square or oval metal band, into the soldering base, will keep the piece upright while it is being soldered. The band should be braced with the joint to the bottom and the solder placed on top of the seam. There is less chance of melting the band, especially one of thin metal (except for very small ones, such as in chain work). Also, any overloading of solder is usually easier to remove from the outer surface of the joint (See Fig. 67).

Straight steel household or bank pins placed at strategic holding points can be used as a quick method for bracing flat pieces. Fine iron binding wire can be wrapped several times around irregular shaped pieces to hold the joints in place when other braces cannot be used (Fig. 68). The method should be chosen according to the shape of the piece to be soldered.

D. Fluxing. Apply flux to all areas to be joined. This material, when heated to a high temperature, forms a glaze which provides protection from oxidation for a limited period of time. In many cases, the fluxed area must be confined to the joint itself, especially when there are mobile touching areas nearby, such as in chain work. If the flux is applied so that it encompasses other touching parts of the chain, as well as the joint being soldered, the solder may flow to all fluxed areas and the chain will become rigid. In cases where touching parts are not a crucial point, as with many larger flat pieces, it is sometimes better to protect the whole piece with flux to help guard against overheating. Again, the jeweler must learn how, with experience, to treat each piece according to its requirements.

Paste fluxes, much as Handy Flux, give longer protection from heat than liquid fluxes, though each has its own particular advantages. For general use, it is probably best to start with a paste. Avoid contamination; dirty flux can prevent solder flow.

E. Solder. In most instances, it is wiser to use more small pieces of solder than fewer large pieces. Smaller pieces melt faster, providing a greater protection against overheating. This, of course, depends on the type of joint being soldered. *Always* use snippets smaller than the work to avoid melting the work itself, as, for example, with fine wire.

Solder can leave an imprint (a slight etching), after flowpoint, wherever it has been placed. This should be removed by mechanical means — by hand sanding, using abrasive tools in a motorized handpiece, or with a flat graver in hard-to-reach areas.

Solder will follow the greatest concentration of heat. Therefore, its flow can be controlled to some extent by guidance with the torch flame.

PICKLING

It cannot be overemphasized that the joint to be soldered must be clean. Previously heated metal should be cleaned of oxides before and after soldering or resoldering it. This is done either mechanically, or, more commonly, by immersing the metal in a hot or boiling pickling solution. It is then rinsed thoroughly in water. Sparex No. 2 is comparatively safe pickle to use for silver and copper. Avoid contact with the skin as it does sting a bit. Directions for mixing with water are on the container. A pickle which can be used for either gold or silver is a mixture of 1 part sulphuric acid mixed with 10 parts cold water. *The water must be measured out first and the acid carefully added to it. If water is added to the acid, dangerous spattering can occur.* A copper pan and a controlled hot plate can be used to heat both of the pickles mentioned above. They can be used cold, but take far longer to clean. I usually bring the solution to a boil with the hot plate set on high, then reduce the temperature setting to medium. If I have other things to do while a piece is in the pickling solution, I set the heat control on low. By the time I am finished working the other piece, the one being pickled is usually clean and ready for the next step.

Store leftover solutions in pyrex or stoneware jars. Rinse copper pans after each use to prevent corrosion. Sulphuric and nitric acids are both potentially hazardous and beginners are advised to seek experienced supervision before attempting to use them in pickling solutions. They can cause serious burns if splashed on the skin. Any part of the body that has been touched by these acids should be flooded with water *immediately*. The fumes are dangerous to breathe.

ANNEALING

When metal is worked in any way — bent, pounded, twisted, rolled or drawn — it soon becomes hard and brittle. If it is not annealed periodically, it will eventually crack. Before starting to anneal, darken your work area; turn off the lights and close the window shades so that you may get a truer view of the glow of the metal as it is being heated. *TO ANNEAL STERLING SILVER*, heat the metal with a torch until the first signs of dull red appear, then *quickly* immerse it in cold water. *TO ANNEAL YELLOW GOLD*, heat to a cherry red, then leave on a charcoal block to cool a few moments before quenching in cold water. Annealing will restore the soft malleable qualities of these metals so that they are ready for further working. It is a good idea, also, to anneal new metals before starting to use them.

Practice Project No. 4

This wire and disc design will give you experience in annealing, soldering and pickling. Tools and supplies needed are: torch, charcoal block, flux and solder, flat nose and chain nose pliers, needle files, jeweler's saw, copper tongs, sanding cloth or paper (medium to very fine grits), sterling round wire (12 and 14 gauge), 12 gauge sterling sheet (about 1 inch), Sparex No. 2.

The Project. 1. Cut wires and discs to the pattern (Fig. 69), allowing for bending, scrolling and joint shaping. 2. Anneal the 14 gauge wire (to be scrolled) and the longest piece of 12 gauge wire (to be bent). 3. Pickle to clean, then rinse in clear water. 4. Bend the longest wire (A) to fit the darkened area of the pattern, using chain nose and flat nose pliers, after first filing halfway through the bend joints with a square needle file (see drawing). 5. Arrange the pieces on a soldering base and brace with pins, etc., avoiding soldering areas. 6. Flux all joints, including the bends, and apply tiny snippets of medium solder to the top of each joint. 7. Heat the whole piece to bring all the solder to flow point at the same time. 8. Allow a few moments to cool, then immerse the piece in hot or boiling pickling solution until clean. Use *only copper or brass*

Fig. 69

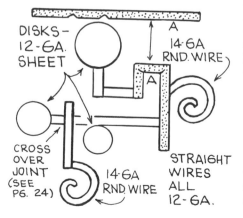

DISKS —
12-6A.
SHEET

A
14-6A
RND. WIRE

A

CROSS
OVER
JOINT
(SEE
PG. 24)

14-6A
RND WIRE

STRAIGHT
WIRES
ALL
12-6A.

tongs in pickle; tongs of iron or steel will cause a reaction in the solution that will "galvanize" gold or silver with a coating of copper. 9. Rinse in clear water and examine the joints. 10. Repeat soldering steps for any joints that did not take. 11. Sand smooth, first with medium, graduating to very fine grit cloth or paper.

Findings can be added later to convert this project into a brooch. Their application will be detailed at the end of Part 8.

Part 8 – Soldering

In the previous two chapters, we've given you the basics of soldering. Now, here are some specific techniques for different types of work that you will encounter.

JOINTS

Wire to Wire Joints — There are no set rules for solder placement on every piece of work; however, certain things should be kept in mind. The greater mass of solder will flow downward, so place the solder across the top of a vertical joint, when possible. Example—two wires butted together, end to end (Fig. 70, next page).

Parallel Round Wires — Method No. 1 (Fig. 71). Where the wires lie parallel, touching at the sides, first file slight flat surfaces on the touching edges. In this way, more surfaces will be soldered together to form a stronger joint. Place tiny snippets of solder directly on top of the seam, about ¼ inch apart.

Parallel Round Wires — Method No. 2 (Fig. 71). It is sometimes difficult to remove solder etchings from joints such as this and still retain the smooth curve of the wire. Where the design permits, a larger piece of solder is placed at each end of the wires. The heat is concentrated slightly more toward one end than the other, and the molten solder quickly drawn toward the center. This is repeated at the other end of the wires. The etched ends are then turned under to be used on the bottom — or inside, as for a double-wire ring shank.

Wire to Sheet Soldering (Fig. 72). For a horizontal joint, such as a wire to sheet applique, lean the solder snippets against the sides of the wire. The flame is applied mainly to the metal sheet to prevent over-heating the wire. As the solder becomes liquid, it will follow along the length of the fluxed bottom of the wire.

Sheet to Sheet Joints — Sweat Soldering (Fig. 73, Pg. 31). When soldering large surfaces together — or even smaller ones, such as findings or pinbacks — pre-soldering one of the mating surfaces can have its advantages. To do this, the smaller of the mating surfaces is prepared with flux and solder snippets while on a soldering base, and the metal is heated until the solder becomes liquid. The soldered piece is then pickled to clean it and rinsed in clear water. It may require filing, slightly, to level lumpy solder which has not completely melted. Both mating surfaces are then fluxed and placed together on a soldering base, with the smaller piece on top. The metal is heated again to bring the solder to a molten stage. Bright liquid seams will show when the job has been done properly, and the top piece will drop somewhat. This pre-soldering method promotes a faster final solder join, and a cleaner one where small overlays or findings are concerned.

Another method of sheet to sheet soldering is to sandwich small snippets of solder between the two fluxed sheets and heat them to the molten stage, in one operation.

Multiple Joins (Fig. 74). Where several joints are close together, it is sometimes best to start the first joint with hard solder, the next with medium solder and a third with easy. Where there are four or more joins, two, or several, can be of medium solder, sandwiched between hard and easy. The distance between and the number of joins will determine which solders to use. Never start with a solder of lower melting point and progress to one with a higher melting point.

USE OF OCHRE (*Fig. 75*)

To help protect a previously soldered joint from melting and collapsing, you can coat it with a water and ochre paste. This paste should then be quickly heat-dried before it can flow into any surrounding flux, causing contamination and preventing solder flow. New joints should be fluxed and heat-dried before applying ochre to previously soldered joints. A joint which has been coated with ochre can still collapse or pit if it becomes overheated. Cleaning with a stiff toothbrush will help to remove remaining ochre after soldering. Immersing in hot pickling solution also helps.

REMOVING OR RELOCATING A JOIN (*Fig. 76*)

There will be times when it is necessary to remove or relocate a solder join. First the work should be pickled thoroughly. Then, the piece must be braced firmly on the soldering base so that it will not move about. The whole piece should be refluxed and dried, ochre applied to other soldered joints, and the metal re-heated until the solder reaches a molten stage. Tweezers should be held with the free hand ready to quickly move or separate the pieces.

While soldering, always have a poker or tweezers on hand to help guide pieces which may shift. A long steel needle or nail, embedded in a wood handle (to insulate against heat), or an awl with a wooden handle are good pokers.

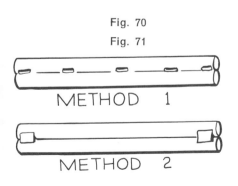

Fig. 70

Fig. 71

METHOD 1

METHOD 2

PARALLEL ROUND WIRE JOINTS

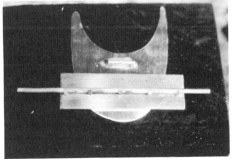

Fig. 72

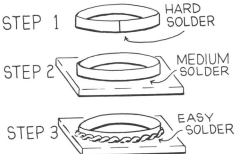

STEP 1 — HARD SOLDER

STEP 2 — MEDIUM SOLDER

STEP 3 — EASY SOLDER

Fig. 73

Fig. 74

Fig. 75

Fig. 76

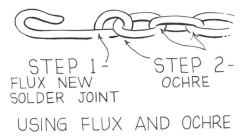

STEP 1 — FLUX NEW SOLDER JOINT   STEP 2 — OCHRE

USING FLUX AND OCHRE

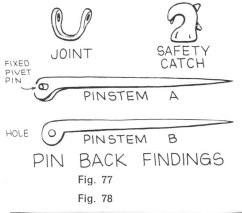

PRACTICE PROJECT NO. 5

Application of Pin Back Findings

Tools and Supplies — small hammer; anvil; pin back findings (safety catch, joint and pinstem as shown in Fig. 77); Project No. 4 brooch; easy solder; medium to very fine sanding cloth or paper; crocus cloth (a very fine abrasive cloth that produces a soft polish — available at many hardware stores and from jewelry and rock hobby suppliers).

The Project

1. Pre-solder the bottoms of the safety catch and joint. Do this after partially opening the catch and pressing the tops of both findings into a magnesia or charcoal soldering block (Fig. 78). Use care when applying the flux so that it covers only the bottom; it must not run into the catch mechanism.

2. Flatten the soldered bottoms slightly, if necessary with a flat file.

3. On the back of the brooch, flux

JOINT

SAFETY CATCH

FIXED PIVET PIN

PINSTEM   A

HOLE

PINSTEM   B

PIN BACK FINDINGS

Fig. 77

Fig. 78

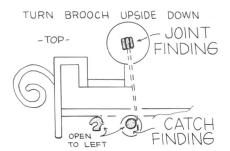

TURN BROOCH UPSIDE DOWN

-TOP-

JOINT
FINDING

OPEN
TO LEFT

CATCH
FINDING

PLACEMENT OF PIN BACK FINDINGS

Fig. 79

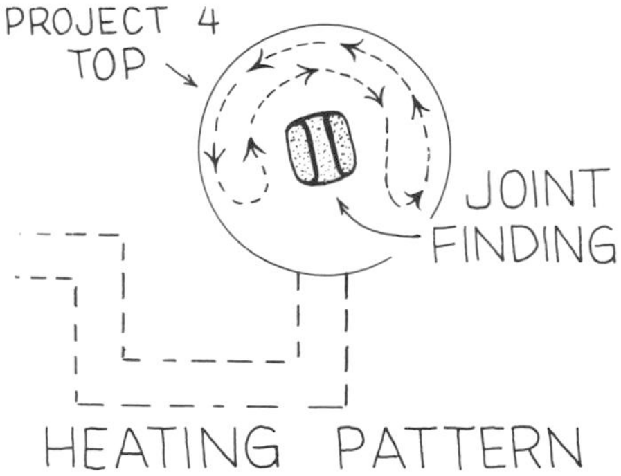

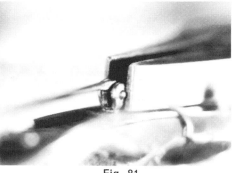

PROJECT 4
TOP

JOINT
FINDING

HEATING PATTERN

Fig. 80

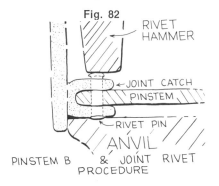

Fig. 81

Fig. 82

RIVET
HAMMER

JOINT CATCH
PINSTEM

RIVET PIN

ANVIL

PINSTEM B & JOINT RIVET
PROCEDURE

the mating areas for the joint and catch (Fig. 79) and torch dry quickly. Holding the brooch with tweezers over the soldering base, apply a paste of yellow ochre to the solder joints close to the mating areas and heat-dry quickly.

4. Flux only the bottoms of the catch and joint findings.

5. Place the brooch, bottom side up on a soldering base.

6. Position the joint and catch findings as shown in Fig. 79. The joint is always to the top and the catch to the bottom. In case the pinstem should come open, there will be less danger of losing the brooch. Slant the joint so that the pinstem points to the back (closed side) of the catch. This will help keep the pin sprung in place in case the catch should open.

7. Concentrate the torch flame in an arc pattern around the joint finding, but not touching it (Fig. 80). Avoid other solder joints.

8. Repeat for the catch finding using a small flame carefully. This soldering is more difficult because of the smaller base; it will test your ability.

9. Pickle and rinse the brooch, then polish the surface with crocus cloth.

10. If the pinstem is too long, measure it and cut off the pointed end so that the pin will extend only 1/16 to 1/8 inch beyond the catch finding (never beyond the edge of the brooch). File the end to a point, then sand with medium, fine and very fine sanding cloth. Polish with crocus cloth.

11. Place the fixed rivet pins of the pinstem in the holes in the joint finding with the flat side of the pinstem to the top. Squeeze the joint finding sides close to the pinstem with chain nose or flat pliers (Fig. 81).

Note: If pinstem B is used, a close fitting wire (rivet pin) must be inserted through the joint and pinstem holes. Both ends of the wire must be flattened over the holes with a small hammer, preferably a rivet hammer, while the joint is held on an anvil (Fig. 82).

Part 9 — Polishing and Coloring

POLISHING

The secret to a beautifully polished piece of jewelry is the strict attention given to each of the preparatory steps leading to final buffing: 1. Soldering must be done correctly, leaving a smooth joint and no excess oxidation or pitting. 2. The piece must be cleaned of surface oxides after soldering or heating, either by pickling, sanding or both. If not completely removed, oxides (fire scale) will show up when the piece is buffed, appearing as gray, cloudy areas. If this happens, and the piece has not been too badly burned, the fire scale can be removed by further sanding. 3. In final preparation, the metal is given a sanded finish, with emery or carborundum paper or cloth, progressing from medium to very fine grits. This should leave a smooth, even finish (the coarseness of the grit with which you start depends on how work scarred the piece has become).

This author prefers to use three compounds for polishing, in the following order: 1. *Tripoli*, a cutting compound, on a felt or muslin buff. 2. *Yellow Platinum Rouge*, a fast polishing compound, on a fine muslin wheel. 3. *Red Rouge*, for a final high luster, on a cotton flannel buff. These compounds can also be used with felt-or leather-covered sticks for polishing by hand. Recommended "midget" wheel buffs (Fig. 83) for use in motorized handpieces are: for tripoli, felt wheels in a variety of sizes and shapes; for yellow rouge, felt or fine muslin; for red rouge, cotton flannel or chamois.

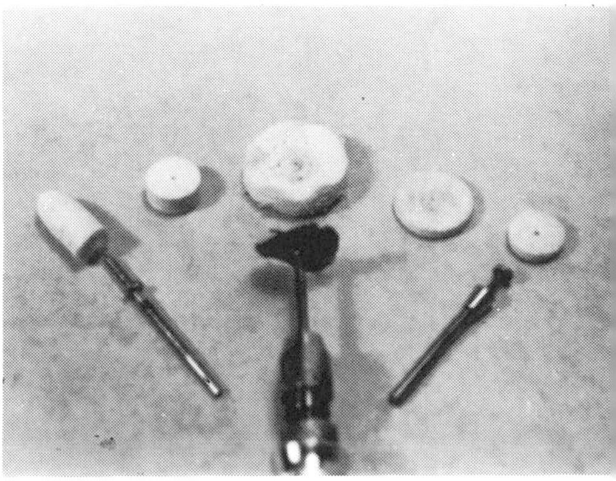

A polishing wheel of felt, cloth or chamois can be charged with polishing compound by chucking it in the motorized handpiece and rotating at fast speed while holding the compound (it comes in cakes or sticks) to the buff. Do not use too much compound or it will tend to drag and build up on the metal. Hand buffing sticks can be charged by drawing them swiftly back and forth across the compound.

It is essential that each buffing wheel or stick be used for one particular compound and kept separate from the others to prevent contamination. A good way

Fig. 83

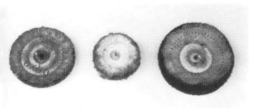

Fig. 84

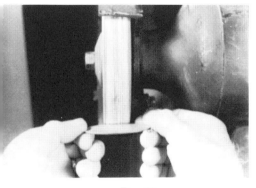

Fig. 85

Fig. 86

to keep the larger (3- to 5-inch) wheels handy and separate is to hang them on 8 penny finishing nails, one for each wheel (Fig. 84).

When using the double spindle polisher with larger wheels, *care must be taken to hold the jewelry firmly and at correct angles.* Buff the work, while holding it angled down, on the lower third of the wheel (Fig. 85). Never work a piece near its top edge or at the center or top of the wheel. The buff can catch hold of the metal with great force, damage or completely ruin it, and injure the person as well.

Considerable pressure should be exerted while polishing. As with sanding, cross over previous directions of buffing where possible. Never polish in one spot only; keep either the piece or the buffing wheel moving, depending on the equipment being used.

Things to Remember

1. Always clean the metal thoroughly and rinse in clear water between each polishing step.

2. Liquid detergent, used full strength, is a good cleaner. Another is detergent, ammonia and warm water.

3. A soft brush aids in cleaning (Fig. 86). *Note: Polishing equipment is decribed in more detail in Part 4.*

COLORING

Jewelry which has multiple overlays, wire appliques, pierced overlays or other decorations can often be given more depth and dimension by color processing. One of the most common processes for coloring silver is to darken it by oxidizing with liver of sulfur, which has been dissolved in water (1/2-inch lump to 1 to 2 pints water) or other commercial solutions. A darker finish can be obtained if the metal or the solution is preheated. Metal which is too hot, or a solution which is too hot or too strong, will cause the color to flake off, so do not use a boiling solution or heat the metal beyond the point of the first sizzle when liquid is applied to it. The color can be painted on with a brush if the piece is small, or the jewelry can be dipped in a container of warmed solution. In Fig. 87, water was first heated in a metal pot, then mixed with liver of sulfur in a pyrex bowl.

When the desired shade is reached, the metal should be rinsed thoroughly to stop the coloring action. It can then be buffed or rubbed with moistened pumice to bring out the highlights.

More Things to Remember

1. Fire scale will prevent uniform coloring and must be removed first.

2. The piece must be cleaned of all oils from polishing compounds, hands, etc., before applying coloring solutions.

Fig. 87

3. Apply color only after all soldering and sanding have been completed.

PRACTICE PROJECT NO. 6
A Ring with Pierced Overlay (Fig. 88)

Tools and Supplies — jeweler's saw, flat hand file, solid ring mandrel, rawhide mallet, 2 pairs pliers (i.e. round nose, chain nose or flat nose), sanding cloth, coloring solution, 20 gauge sterling sheet.

Fig. 88

Fig. 89

The Project (Figs. 89, 90 and 91)

A. (See drawing). Make a pattern for the ring finger by fitting a band of paper of the desired width around the large knuckle. Hold in place tightly and cut the ends to meet.

B. Place this pattern on a 20 gauge sterling sheet and scribe lightly around it. Allow a small margin for filing smooth. Also, make an allowance in the length of the band for the difference between the thickness of the paper pattern and the metal. A rule of thumb is to add about half the thickness of the metal. In this case, half the thickness of the double-layered band equals the thickness of one 20 gauge sheet. Add this amount, about 1/16 inch, to the length. Duplicate this step (B) to make two identical strips.

C. Cut out the metal strips with the jeweler's saw. Smooth the edges with a flat hand file and file the ends perfectly straight.

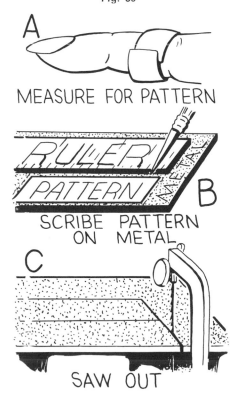

A MEASURE FOR PATTERN

B SCRIBE PATTERN ON METAL

C SAW OUT

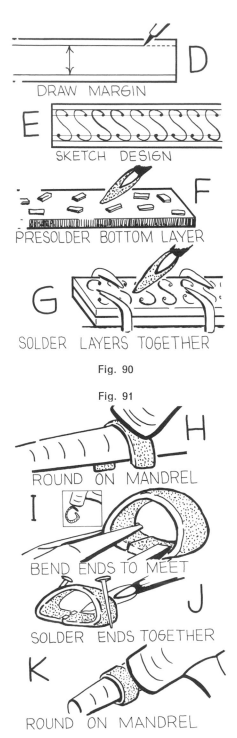

DRAW MARGIN

SKETCH DESIGN

PRESOLDER BOTTOM LAYER

SOLDER LAYERS TOGETHER

Fig. 90

Fig. 91

ROUND ON MANDREL

BEND ENDS TO MEET

SOLDER ENDS TOGETHER

ROUND ON MANDREL

D. Draw a small margin along the long edges of one of the metal strips.

E. Sketch a series of identical S's inside the center margin. Place the metal over a block of wood and, with a center punch or nail, make a dent at both ends of each S, then drill a small hole in each indentation. Insert the jeweler's saw blade through one hole and saw carefully along the lines of the S to the other drilled hole. Repeat for each S.

F. Flux, then presolder the top surface of the unpierced strip, using medium solder. Pickle and rinse. Flux the mating surfaces of both strips.

G. Secure the strips, layered together, on a soldering base and heat with the torch until the solder flows. Pickle and rinse. With the flat hand file, true up any edges that may not be flush.

H. With the rawhide mallet and fingers, partially round the band around a solid ring mandrel.

I. Using two pairs of smooth-jawed pliers, and a rawhide mallet, bend the ends toward each other, then spring them past each other until they stay tightly and evenly together.

J. Secure the band upright on a soldering base, with the seam to the bottom. Flux all surfaces. Place easy solder snippets along the seam. Bring the solder to flowpoint with the torch. Pickle and rinse.

K. True the ring by placing it on the ring mandrel and rounding with blows of the rawhide mallet. (The band can be enlarged to a certain degree by more pounding with the mallet while on the mandrel.) File the outer surface smooth with a flat hand file, then sand all surfaces of the band, graduating from medium to very fine cloth. Rinse in water to remove abrasives and dry. Polish according to previous instructions. Small drum sanding tools and small felt wheels in a motorized handpiece deliver faster finishing on the inside of the band.

Color the band according to directions on pages 34 and 35. Repolish with red rouge to remove color from all surfaces except the pierced design.

Part 10 — Stone Setting

By Iva L. Geisinger
Salinas, California

As you gain experience and knowledge in creating jewelry from wire and sheet metal, you will undoubtedly wish to incorporate cut and polished stones in many of your designs. While you are learning how to set gems, learn also their names, hardness and other characteristics, as well as the name of the shape or cut. This will not only enrich your background knowledge, thereby making it more interesting, but will also give you a broader perspective when designing a jewelry piece.

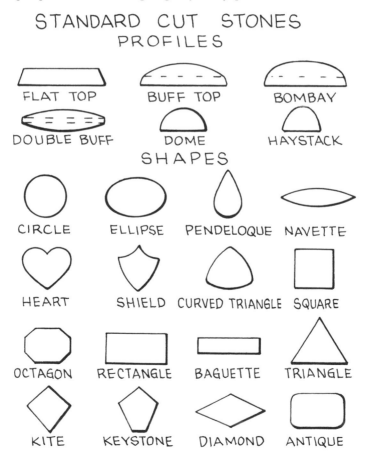

STANDARD CUT STONES
PROFILES

FLAT TOP   BUFF TOP   BOMBAY

DOUBLE BUFF   DOME   HAYSTACK

SHAPES

CIRCLE   ELLIPSE   PENDELOQUE   NAVETTE

HEART   SHIELD   CURVED TRIANGLE   SQUARE

OCTAGON   RECTANGLE   BAGUETTE   TRIANGLE

KITE   KEYSTONE   DIAMOND   ANTIQUE

10° TO 15° BEVEL ANGLE

Fig. 92

Fig. 93

Fig. 94

Fig. 95

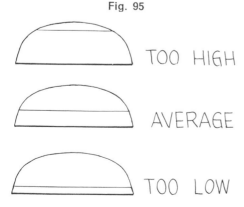

TOO HIGH

AVERAGE

TOO LOW

BEZEL SET STONES

Bezel wire is used to construct bezel boxes, generally for the setting of cabochons. It is produced flat or with a shelf (seat) for the stone to rest upon. Start with 26 gauge (thickness), fine silver, *flat* bezel wire for use with most medium sized stones. This wire can be purchased by the foot at many rock shops and from catalog suppliers. I advise the beginner to start with this flat type and add built-up designs (beading, twists, etc.). Later, you may wish to try the bezel wire with built-in designs which is also available from the suppliers.

Note: For best results, use cabochons with 10°-15° slope (Fig. 92).

Basic Bezel — Round Cabochons

1. Turn the stone upside down and fit the bezel wire around its bottom edge to form a collar (Fig. 93). Cut away excess wire, allowing extra length for filing the ends smooth and straight. When the ends of the collar are held together, the stone should be able to just drop *straight* through.

2. Hard solder the ends together. Use the soldering techniques from Parts 6, 7 and 8.

3. Round the collar on a bezel mandrel or other small round rod, using a rawhide mallet (Fig. 94).

4. Again, push the stone through the collar. If it cannot be passed straight through easily, the collar is too small. If this happens, place it over a bezel mandrel or other round rod, and tap it lightly with a small hammer until the correct enlargement is achieved.

5. Even the collar's bottom by rubbing it over medium grit emery paper on a flat surface.

6. Re-check to see that the collar is still aligned to the shape of the stone.

7. Solder the bezel collar to its base (bola slide, belt buckle, etc.), with medium or easy solder.

8. File the top of the bezel to a height which looks well with the particular

stone being used. Too high a bezel will wrinkle when it is being pressed against the gem; one that is too low will not have enough holding power. The bezel must bend over enough of the stone to hold it securely (Fig. 95).

9. Sand and polish (Part 5, Page 20 and Part 9).

Basic Bezel — Oval Cabochon

Follow the directions for round stones, except, in place of Step 3, use the fingers to true the bezel, by molding it directly around the stone's lower edge. Other methods are shown in Fig. 96.

Square, Rectangular and Other Sharply Angled Bezels

1. Starting about halfway on one side, fit the bezel wire around the gem's under edge, while holding the stone upside down. To do a sharp 90° turn, make a *slight* cut along the first corner line with the jeweler's saw or a knife edge file (Fig. 97A), then use flat nose pliers to bend the wire (Fig. 97B). Proceed in the same way around each corner until ends of the bezel wire overlap. Cut away excess wire, leaving some extra material to file straight and smooth and to a proper fit. Again, the stone must slip through the collar without binding.

2. Hard solder the saw-notched corners, as well as the meeting ends of the bezel collar (Fig. 98).

3. Follow steps 5, 6 and 7 for a basic bezel for round cabochons.

4. After soldering to a base, file V's at the top of each corner of the bezel with a knife edge needle file (Fig. 99A). The length of the V needed will will depend on the slant of the stone — the greater the angle, the longer the V. Usually a cut of at least 2/3 to ¾ of the bezel height will be required to allow the bezel to be pressed securely against the stone without puckering at the corners. Round the tops of the V's with a barrette file (Fig. 99B).

5. Finish as for a round bezel.

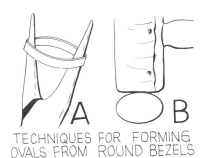

TECHNIQUES FOR FORMING OVALS FROM ROUND BEZELS

Fig. 96

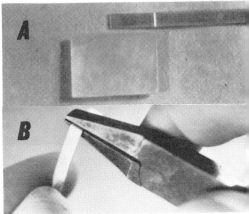

Fig. 97

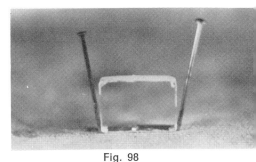

Fig. 98

Fig. 99

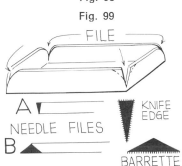

BEZEL WITH INSERTED BASE

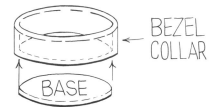

BEZEL COLLAR

BASE

BASE SCRIBED AND FILED
TO FIT INSIDE COLLAR.

Fig. 100

BEARING BEZEL

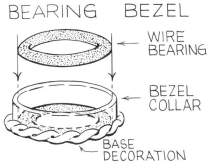

WIRE BEARING

BEZEL COLLAR

BASE DECORATION

Fig. 101

BEZEL WITH CURVED BASE

BEARING

Fig. 102

Fig. 103

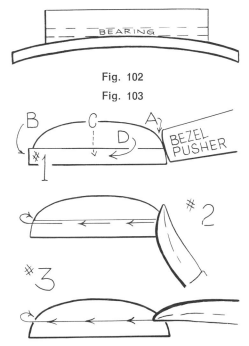

BEZEL PUSHER

#1

#2

#3

Bezel with Inserted Base (Fig. 100)

In some cases the bezel should be made with an inserted base (a flat piece fitted inside and flush with the bottom of the collar). This method is used when a stone is to be displayed without raised decoration. If a bezel collar is soldered to a base of the same diameter, in time the solder will oxidize faster than the rest of the piece and reveal a faint line.

Bezel with Bearing (Fig. 101)

When a raised decoration, such as beaded or twisted wire, etc., is to be used around the base of the bezel, a wire bearing should be inserted and soldered inside and to the bottom, in order to raise the stone above the decoration level (or use manufactured bezel wire with a bearing). This will allow the extra height needed for a proper setting, with little or no filing of the bezel top. Bearings can be made from round wire for round bezels and square wire for square ones, the gauge to depend on the height of the decoration. Also, use a bezel with a bearing over a curved base (Fig. 102), filing the bottom to fit the base.

Setting a Cabochon (Fig. 103)

1. Push the bezel against the stone with a bezel pusher (also called a stone pusher — available from rock hobby suppliers), working first on one side, then on the opposite side until all the bezel lays smoothly against the stone.

2. Use a burnishing tool (near its tip) to press the top edge close to the stone. Draw the burnisher toward you, applying firm pressure.

3. Finish by drawing the end of the burnishing tool straight across the top of the bezel with controlled pressure, "riveting" the metal to the cabochon.

Carefully remove scratches and re-polish where necessary. A barrette needle file, scotchstone or a rubberized abrasive wheel in a flex-shaft handpiece are suggested aids.

The next section will feature a bezel project for an oval cabochon.

Part 11 — Stone Setting

To become a good jeweler, the beginning student must put his instructions into practice; the more the better. This project incorporates some of the techniques from the preceding chapter on bezel construction for cabochons.

Read the project through and note the tools and supplies required. Figure 104A is the design for Project No. 7. After completing it, try B, C and D, then create designs of your own, building them up from a base.

PROJECT NO. 7
A Ring With A Bezel Set Cabochon

Materials

14 gauge sterling round wire for shank
14 gauge sterling round wire for designs
26 gauge pure silver *flat* bezel wire
20 gauge sterling sheet for design base
1 oval cabochon (a fairly large stone is advised for beginners)

Making the Shank

1. Measure the large knuckle of the ring finger with a narrow strip of paper. Cut away overlapping paper so that ends just meet.

2. Mark this measurement on paper. Add about half the gauge of the shank wire to the length to partially make up for the difference in thickness of the paper pattern and the shank wire (Fig. 105).

3. Place the cabochon at one end of the marked measurement and draw a split-end design, keeping the width of the split ends inside the length of the stone or intended base length (Fig. 106).

4. Cut two lengths of 14 gauge wire about ¾ inch longer than the design dimension. This excess length allows for curving the split shank ends.

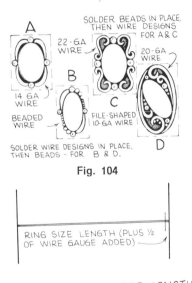

Fig. 104

DRAW PATTERN OF RING SIZE LENGTH

Fig. 105

Fig. 106

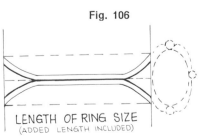

LENGTH OF RING SIZE
(ADDED LENGTH INCLUDED)

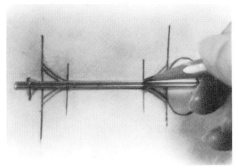

Fig. 107

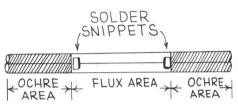

SOLDER
SNIPPETS

OCHRE AREA | FLUX AREA | OCHRE AREA

Fig. 108

Fig. 109

Fig. 110

5. Anneal these wires according to directions, Part 7, Page 28. Pickle and rinse.

6. Straighten them both as perfectly as possible. Use fingers; two pairs of flat nose, smooth jawed pliers; a rawhide mallet or all three, if necessary.

7. Place the wires on the design. Let the wire ends extend equally beyond the design at both ends. Mark across both wires with a soft lead pencil at the points at which the design ends separate (Fig. 107).

8. Secure the wires, close together and even across the top, on a soldering base. Paint between the marked points with a paste of flux. Quickly dry with heat.

9. Apply a paste of yellow ochre to the unfluxed ends of the wires. Dry quickly with heat so that the ochre does not run into the flux and prevent the solder from flowing.

10. Place one fairly large snippet of solder, about 2mm square, at each end of the fluxed area (Fig. 108).

11. Heat the wires with the torch, drawing the solder, as it melts, toward the center with the heat of the flame. Pickle and rinse.

12. Spread the ends of the wires, bending them with your fingers to fit the pattern. Cut off the excess length and file straight across both ends until they are even with the pattern (Fig. 109). File (use needle files) and sand away any solder lumps.

13. With the best surface to the outside, use the fingers to partially round the ring shank around a steel mandrel.

14. Sharply turn the spread ends toward each other, using round nose, then chain nose pliers, until the ends meet. Push them past each other — first one side, then the other, until the ends stay sprung tightly and evenly together (Fig. 110)

15. Hard solder the two joints. Pickle and rinse.

16. True the shank on the ring mandrel with the rawhide mallet This will also enlarge the shank slightly. If a little more enlargement is needed, continue pounding until the correct size is reached. Filing and sanding of work scarred metal on the inside of the band will also enlarge the ring.

17. Flatten the top, straight across the solder lines, with a flat hand file — about half through the wire gauge (Fig. 111). Set aside until the bezel base is completed.

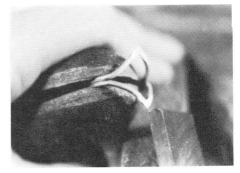
Fig. 111

Bezel, Base and Design

18. Make a bezel collar for the stone as directed in Part 10, with the ends hard soldered together.

19. Flux, then medium solder the collar to a fluxed (both sides) base of 20 gauge sheet which is enough larger than the bezel to accommodate the design. Direct the flame to the underside of the base until the metal begins to turn a greenish color, then heat the top area until the solder flows (Fig. 112). Pickle and rinse.

Fig. 112

20. Sand and polish the bezel collar and the top of the base metal. Clean and rinse with water.

21. Melt short lengths of silver wire on a charcoal block to form the beads for the design. Pickle and rinse them.

22. Usually beads will form with a slightly flattened bottom as they cool. Hold each one deeply between the thumb and forefinger and level this flat area with a square needle file (Fig. 113). Flux the mating areas, then medium solder the beads, flat side down, to the sheet metal base, according to the design (you can pre-solder the flat side of the beads). Be careful not to overheat the thinner bezel wire. Pickle and rinse.

Fig. 113
Fig. 114

23. Bend and file the 14 gauge wire according to the design, fitting the pieces directly to the metal base (Fig. 114). Flux the mating areas, then medium solder all the wire designs in place in one operation. Pickle and rinse.

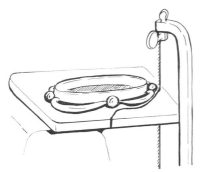

Fig. 115

Fig. 116

Fig. 117

Fig. 118

24. Make a bearing to fit inside the bezel, following the instructions in Part 10, page 40. Flux the mating areas and easy solder in place, carefully to prevent overheating the bezel collar. Pickle and rinse.

25. Saw away the excess on the sheet metal base (Fig. 115). File the edges smooth and close to the design wires.

26. Sand, then polish the underside and edges of the bezel base and outside of the ring shank. Clean with liquid detergent and rinse with water.

27. Flux the top (split side) of the ring shank. Pre-solder the top with easy solder. To promote a smoother coat, use a soldering poker with a spreading motion as the solder begins to flow (Fig. 116). Pickle and rinse.

28. Place the bezel base, topside down, on a magnesia or charcoal block and press into the block. This is to prevent dislocation of the design wires and beads during the new soldering step.

29. Flux the bottom of the bezel base and re-flux the shank top.

30. Center the shank on the base, split side down (Fig. 117).

31. Play the torch back and forth to heat both pieces until the presoldered coating on the shank flows. Pickle and rinse.

32. Fit the stone in the bezel to determine bezel height. If necessary, shorten the bezel by filing evenly across its top with a flat hand file.

33. Sand and polish where needed. Clean thoroughly; use a toothbrush to scrub around the design areas.

34. To bring out the design, apply coloring solution to all the design areas surrounding the bezel (see *Coloring*, Part 9). Repolish the piece to highlight the raised design.

35. Bezel in the stone and finish according to the instructions in Part 10. Figure 118 shows the finished ring.

Part 12 — Stone Setting

By Iva L. Geisinger

SIMPLE PRONG SETTINGS

For Cabochons on a Flat Base (Fig. 119, A and B)

A basic prong setting can be utilized for either cabochon or faceted stones. Here are some methods for cabochons:

A. When a base is used which is the same size as the stone, the edge of the base is notched with a file at each prong site. The notches should have an edge depth of about 1/3 to 1/2 the gauge of the prong wire. Hard solder the prongs into the notches. The inside edges of the prongs are then filed even with the base perimeter.

B. When a base is used which is larger than the stone, the prong spacing can be determined by using the stone as a pattern. Holes can be drilled into the base, and the bottoms of the prongs inserted and hard soldered in them for greater strength.

For Faceted Round Stones (Fig. 120)

This setting is constructed by first soldering together a stone seat of round wire which will fit just under the girdle (the widest part of the gem). Prongs are soldered into notches which have been cut with a joint file about halfway through the outside of the stone seat wire. They should be spaced equally. The prongs should extend above and below the seat — enough above to shape and turn over the edge of the gem's girdle (with a flat nose bezel pusher) — and enough below the seat to act as legs which will be soldered to a base. These legs should be tall enough to hold the culet (lower point of the stone) above the mounting base.

Prong Setting from Tubing (Fig. 121)

One type of prong setting can be made from heavy wall tubing by filing or grinding to make prongs, then spreading the tops of the prongs with a round dapping punch and hammer. A stone seat (shoulder) is notched on the inside of the prongs with a file.

Star Prong Setting (Fig. 122)

This setting is made from sheet metal, sawed to a 5-pointed star shape (A). Slits can be cut from a center hole,

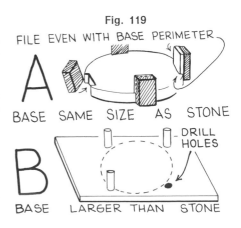

Fig. 119

FILE EVEN WITH BASE PERIMETER

A

BASE SAME SIZE AS STONE

B

DRILL HOLES

BASE LARGER THAN STONE

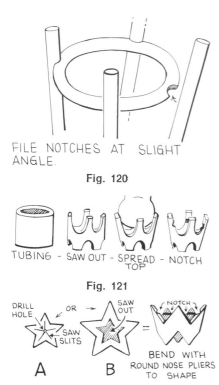

FILE NOTCHES AT SLIGHT ANGLE.

Fig. 120

TUBING - SAW OUT - SPREAD TOP - NOTCH

Fig. 121

DRILL HOLE OR SAW OUT NOTCH

SAW SLITS

A   B   BEND WITH ROUND NOSE PLIERS TO SHAPE

Fig. 122

Fig. 123

Fig. 124

straight toward each point or a small star cut as shown in Fig. 122B, its dimensions depending on the size of the piece. Bend inside points down, outside points up. Experiment with thin copper sheets for approximate pattern sizes.

PRONG SETTINGS FOR RECTANGULAR FACETED STONES PROJECT NO. 8 (FIG. 123)

NOTE: By this time, the reader should be familiar with the basic steps of soldering, sanding, annealing, finishing and polishing. Each step will not be covered individually; just carefully follow through with what you have learned unless special instructions are given.

As a reminder, be sure to anneal all metals to be worked; flux the joining areas before each solder job; pickle and rinse after each soldering step; and clean and rinse the piece, as directed, between each polishing step. Work slowly — speed comes with experience — and think through each step before you attempt it. Read the project through first to determine the tools and supplies needed.

Materials

14 gauge sterling round wire for all construction

1 cut-corner rectangular faceted stone (also known as an octagon cut), 12x16 mm.

Stone Seat and Prongs

1. Construct a stone seat by fitting round 14 gauge sterling wire just under the girdle of the gem. About half the width of the wire should show when the stone is resting on the seat. The corners can be squared better by filing about halfway through at the inside of each one with a square needle file before bending. Do not try to follow the contours of the stone's cut corners. See Fig. 124.

2. Hard solder the joint and each filed and bent corner.

3. File a groove on the inside of each corner with a joint file (about ¾ of the way through) to accommodate the prong wire (Fig. 125).

4. Medium solder the 14 gauge prong wires in the grooves by holding a long length of the wire over a soldering base with soldering tweezers and letting one corner groove of the stone seat balance on the wire toward the opposite end (leave about ¾ inch of wire extended beyond the seat for the prong. See Fig. 126). After soldering, cut away excess wire, leaving about 1/2 inch for the prong leg (¼ inch above, ½ inch below the stone seat). Repeat the soldering procedure for each prong.

5. File the inside corner edge of each prong until the gem rests on the seat (Fig. 127).

Shank Oval

6. Form an oval of 14 gauge round wire to which the prong legs will be soldered. This oval should just fit inside the stone seat (Fig. 128). It should be larger than the table (flat horizontal top surface), yet smaller than the seat. This places it out of focus when viewing the stone from the top. Hard solder the ends of the oval together. Set aside until Step 7 is completed.

7. Measure the large knuckle of the ring finger with a narrow strip of paper and cut away the excess at the overlap. On paper, draw a straight line the length of this pattern, allowing about 3/8 inch extra for fitting and filing smooth (see previous chapter).

8. Center the shank oval on the drawn line. Sketch the shape of the wire design as shown in Fig. 129.

Shank

9. Cut two lengths of 14 gauge round wire longer than the chart length to allow for scrolling and filing even.

10. Straighten the wires as perfectly as possible, so that they fit closely together when secured side by side on a soldering base.

11. Flux the soldering area and ochre the ends which are to be scrolled. Dry quickly with heat after each application.

12. Hard solder the fluxed area. If needed, smooth the groove between the wires with a 3-corner needle file.

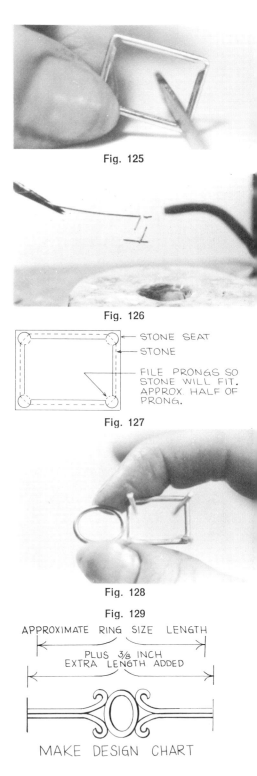

Fig. 125

Fig. 126

STONE SEAT
STONE
FILE PRONGS SO STONE WILL FIT. APPROX HALF OF PRONG.

Fig. 127

Fig. 128

Fig. 129

APPROXIMATE RING SIZE LENGTH

PLUS ⅜ INCH EXTRA LENGTH ADDED

MAKE DESIGN CHART

13. Saw the wire shank into two pieces of equal length. Spread and scroll the unsoldered ends to match your design, with fingers and round nose pliers (see Fig. 129).

14. With all the pieces laying flat on a soldering base, align the scrolled ends of the shank to both sides of the oval. File a slight flat area at touching points. Medium solder all joints in one operation (Fig. 130).

15. Choosing the best side for the outside, round the shank section around a numbered ring mandrel with the fingers and a rawhide mallet. Overlap the ends and mark both shanks at the center of the overlap. Cut to allow extra length, then file smooth and even to the correct size.

16. Bend and fit the shank ends together as described in Part 11, then medium solder the joint (Fig. 131).

17. True the shank on the ring mandrel with a rawhide mallet.

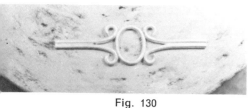

Fig. 130

Fig. 131

18. Curve the lower legs of the prong section inward with round nose pliers, and file to fit the top of the shank oval. (Legs should be longer than necessary to begin with.) Reduce excess length by filing evenly across all four at once. Continue filing, bending and fitting the legs, until the culet of the stone is just above the top of the ring shank. The stone seat should be level when viewing it from all sides.

19. Center the prong and leg section to the top of the shank oval, and easy solder in place (Fig. 132).

20. The prongs should be about half the thickness of the 14 gauge wire. If thinning is needed for easier bending, file and sand them around their outer halves. Shorten the tops, leaving just enough to bend securely over the stone's girdle. Round the tops with a file.

21. Sand and polish the ring. Hard-to-reach areas can be done with a cotton-tipped matchstick, charged with polishing compound and inserted in a flexshaft handpiece.

Fig. 132

Fig. 133

Setting the Stone

22. At one end, slightly bend over two of the prongs with round nose pliers. Set the stone on its seat, slipping it under the bent prongs first. Bend the straight prongs over the gem with a burnishing tool, or by mounting the ring over a tissue-covered mandrel and *gently* tapping the prongs securely over the edge of the stone with a flat nose bezel pusher and hammer (Fig. 133). Reverse the ring on the mandrel and tap the opposite prongs, as needed.

Part 13 — Chain Making

Once one learns how to quickly make chain links, it is then an easy step to incorporate those links in many styles of chains. Round or oval links, also known as jump rings, can be used to connect other components together, such as forged or scrolled wire pieces. Square and rectangular links can also be developed into interesting chains.

HOW TO FORM LINKS

Round Links

1. Clamp the end of a short length of wood dowling of the required diameter in a bench vise. Steel rods or nails with heads removed can also be used.

2. Select the gauge of wire to be used and cut it to the approximate length needed. Coil it loosely, anneal, pickle and rinse (Fig. 134).

3. Coil the wire tightly around the dowling in a slightly overlapping movement. Each coil should touch the next (Fig. 135). Maintain a good tension until the desired amount of links are wound. Remove the dowel and coils from the vise.

4. Use the jeweler's saw, with a fine tooth blade, to cut *straight* through one side of the wound coil (Fig. 136).

5. Before incorporating the links into chains, or using them otherwise, gently remove the tiny burs left by the saw with a needle file (Fig. 137). So that you may reach the link ends with the file, force them apart *sideways*, not by further opening.

Oval Links

1. Coil the wire around two nails (with heads removed) that have been driven into wood (Fig. 138).

2. Or, wind the wire around a rectangular rod. It will retain curves and form ovals.

Fig. 134

Fig. 135

Square or Rectangular Links

Use a square or rectangular rod, tapping the wire with a mallet to conformity as it is being wound.

Making a Round or Oval Link Chain

1. Follow the directions for making links.

Fig. 136

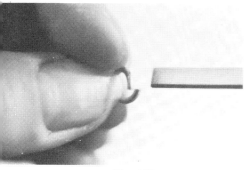

Fig. 137

Fig. 138

Fig. 139

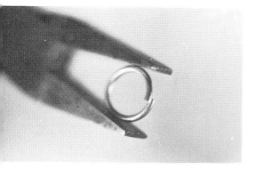

2. Close and solder half the links needed for a chain as follows:

a. With flat nose pliers, squeeze each link so that the ends go slightly past each other (Fig. 139).

b. Force the ends back a little and twist them slightly so that they spring together. Repeat if necessary; they should fit snugly and evenly.

c. Lay the links flat on a soldering base, flux each joint and hard solder with tiny pieces of solder.

3. Connect each of the remaining open links to the soldered links, following with steps a and b.

4. Pin the links to the soldering base (in total or by long sections, depending on the length of the chain). Face each unsoldered joint to the top or front (Fig. 140). Apply an ochre paste to touching areas close to the joints. Dry quickly with heat. Apply flux to the unsoldered joints and dry quickly.

5. Solder with hard solder.

6. Dip in cool water.

7. Repeat Step 4 for long chains.

8. Pickle and rinse when completed.

9. Polish the chain. This can be done by charging a soft cloth with tripoli, enfolding the chain in it and rubbing both between the fingers (Fig. 141).

Or, chain can be wound around heavy cardboard and firmly attached or gripped, then held to a polishing wheel and carefully buffed. It should *never* be held by itself in the fingers to be polished, as it can, and generally does, become wound around the wheel, is usually ruined, and often injures the person doing the work.

FORGING

This is a method of forming metal by hammering — to cup, stretch, shape, draw in, and planish it.

The following project introduces the beginning jeweler to simple forging procedures. Forged units are connected with oval and round links to form a chain. The chain holds a pendant with mobile parts which, in turn, are attached by tiny round links.

PENDANT WITH MOBILE UNITS AND CHAIN (Fig. 143)
Materials — Also See Fig. 144

18 gauge sheet — pendant frames
14 gauge square wire — mobile units
18 gauge square wire — top mobile units
12 gauge round wire — center linking components and chain units
16 gauge round wire — chain links
22 gauge round wire — mobile unit links
1 square cabochon — 15mm
1 round cabochon — 11mm diameter

Fig. 140

1. *CHAIN* — Measure for the desired length and draw a straight line that long on paper. Allowing for the width of the pendant, divide the chain area into link and component parts, and determine how many of each will be needed.

2. *FRAMES* — From solid sterling sheet, saw the two frames, including cross bars, etc. Sawed edges should be filed smooth. The frames' surface texture is achieved with a small hammer and round dapping tool (any round steel ball about the size of a small marble can be utilized). Practice on a copper sheet first, tapping the tool or steel ball with the hammer, forming slightly overlapping dents.

Fig. 141

3. *MOBILE UNITS* — These are forged round wires. Strike the portion of the wires shown flattened in the pattern, sharply, on an anvil until the metal flattens to the desired width (Fig. 142).

4. *DRILLING* — Use very small drill bits — Nos. 1 and 2, round. Counter punch first and fill the dent with a drop of light lubricant, such as sewing machine oil or 3-In-One and drill through the oil. This acts as a coolant for the bit and speeds the work; your drill bit will stay sharp longer.

5. *FINISHING* — Do not try to smooth all surfaces of the forged pieces. First, use a fine wire brush by hand or in a motorized handpiece. The object for this piece of jewelry is to retain the interesting textures created by forging. After wire brushing, any rough edges

Fig. 142

Fig. 143

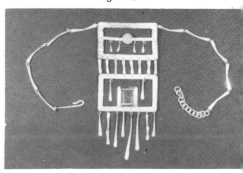

should be smoothed by sanding or with rubberized abrasive tools. Round the ends if necessary. Then all pieces can be individually polished with tripoli before assembling.

6. *ASSEMBLING* — Assemble the pieces according to the pattern, using techniques already learned. The weight and mobile structure of the necklace requires that *all* links be soldered. This is difficult on the small ones, but excellent practice. Use a small flame and lots of patience. Repolish all surfaces with yellow rouge. Do not try for a high finish. This piece will look better with only a soft polish.

7. *SET THE STONES* — Many commercial square gems come with straight, instead of angled sides. In this case, bezels should be the same height as the stone so that the top edges can be rolled just over the upper curve of the gem. Bezel corners are mitered only slightly and are crimped around the cabochon corners. Thinning the top edge of the bezel will aid in setting the stone. See Part 10 for details on square bezels for angled cabochons.

Fig. 144

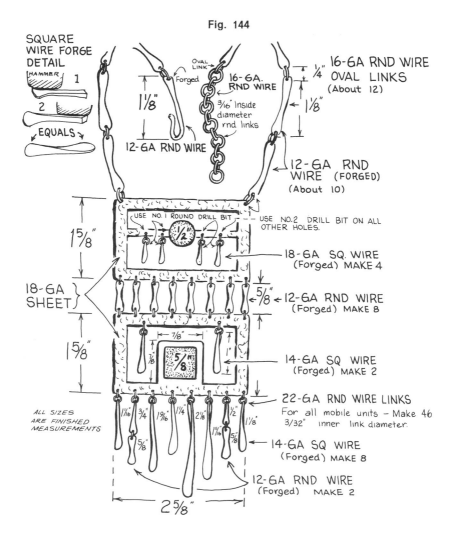

Part 14 — Decorative Techniques

Forming, Chasing and Stamping

Metal can be given added interest, depth and reflection with several working techniques. To produce slight *form* or *contour*, it can be bent either with the fingers or by tapping it lightly with a rawhide mallet over a lead sheet, or use smooth-jawed round nose pliers or bending pliers. It can also be formed into different convex or concave shapes with punches and a broad faced hammer. This can be done by embedding the annealed metal in a pitchbowl or by working it over a sheet of lead. The methods are explained further in the next few paragraphs.

Metal can also be decorated by chasing line designs and by stamping it with graining or matting tools. Remember, it should be annealed before beginning to work and frequently while working to prevent cracking.

LEAD SHEET as a forming base — check with a plumbing supply as a possible source of sheet lead, or make a sheet by melting scrap lead into a *dry*, shallow pan. The sheet needn't be more than 7 to 9 inches square by about 3/8 to ½ inch thick.

First indent into the lead the shape desired (Fig. 145A), then place the metal over the indentation. With the hammer and punch, rapidly tap the metal into the indented contours of the lead, keeping the tool moving constantly (Fig. 145B).

PITCHBOWL (Fig. 146) — This is also a handy item to have and is especially good for doing repousse work (covered below). Pitchbowls can be purchased from jeweler's supply houses already filled with a special pitch mixture consisting of approximately 3 parts pitch, 2 parts plaster of Paris and 2 parts tallow. The bowl should be used while resting in a ring type of base, usually a heavy wooden one. This permits it to be tipped for the best working position. To work with metal in pitch, it is slowly and carefully heated with a soft flame (use a large, no. 3 tip) until it softens. It can then be domed up in the center of the bowl to make working on the metal more convenient. While the pitch is soft, press the metal into it so that the pitch is

Fig. 145

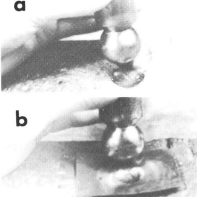

a

b

Fig. 146

Fig. 147

Fig. 148
Fig. 149

flush with the top of the metal. Then push up a little of the pitch slightly over the edges of the metal to secure it (Fig. 147). It can then be cooled with running water.

To remove worked metal from the pitchbowl, carefully heat the surrounding pitch until pliable and the piece can easily be pried up at the edges. Any pitch that adheres to the metal can be burned to a white ash with the torch. Applying oil to metal first will help prevent pitch from sticking to it.

REPOUSSE

This is a method of raising sheet metal into relief forms from the underside. Chasing tools and assorted rounded punches are used. The work can be done on a pitchbowl, lead sheet or hardwood.

A pitchbowl is an ideal base for creating repousse. The pitch is heated and the metal secured in it, with the outlined design scribed on the top. The design detail can then be delineated (Fig. 148A) with a *line chasing* tool called a *tracer* (see *Chasing* below). The lines should be chased deep enough to show a faint ridge on the bottom (Fig. 148B). The piece can then be turned over and the relief work carried on within the ridged lines of the design (Fig. 149).

The metal is then removed, turned over and secured to hardwood (with small nails around the edges) so that the background around relief forms can be smoothed and flattened with modeling tools (Fig. 150). For a concave background, it can be turned over, embedded in the pitch and worked. Modeling tools are flat or slightly rounded.

Sharper delineation can also be carried out at this time. Relief and background steps are repeated until the desired effect is achieved.

CHASING

This is basically the art of using tools to line and define; stamping with curved and angled line punches, making sharp, single blows with a hammer; modeling with flat or convex tipped tools; and giving metal interesting surface texture with matting or graining tools.

Lines can be chased onto metal sheet with the sheet secured on hardwood or a pitchbowl. The lining (tracing) tool is held by the thumb, first and second fingers. The remaining two fingers should act as a brace, with the little finger gliding smoothly along the work surface as the line work progresses. The tool should be tipped backward slightly so that the rapid tapping of the hammer on its top will push it steadily forward as it forms a grooved line (Fig. 151).

When using a pitchbowl for line work, tilt it slightly away from you and work the line toward yourself. Practice on 16 to 18 gauge copper sheet until you can incise a smooth, unbroken line without "stitches" (overlapping or crossing lines). Use the first two fingers to guide the tool. Practice curved as well as straight lines.

Some Chasing Tools

Lining tools (Fig. 152A)
Repousse tools (Fig. 152B)
Modeling tools (Fig. 152C)

Making Your Own Chasing Tools

Many chasing tools can be made in your own shop. Purchase 1/8-to ½-inch *tool steel* rod stock — round, square or rectangular. Saw, or have it sawed into 4-to 5-inch lengths. Shape the end of a rod into the kind of tool desired (see Fig. 152) with a coarse, then a fine cut file. Slightly blunt the working edges of line making tools so that they will not cut metal too much. Sand the working faces of the tool, graduating from coarse to very fine. Polish as for jewelry, using high speed equipment, about 3450 r.p.m., if possible.

Harden the working faces by heating the bottom half inch of the tool to a cherry red and *quenching immediately* in cold water. Repolish the tip. Temper by reheating about an inch above the working faces until the tip reaches a wheat or dark yellow color, then immediately requenching. Again, polish the tool and it is ready for use.

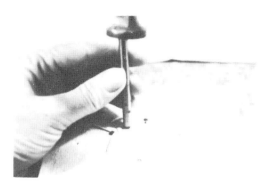

Fig. 150

Fig. 151

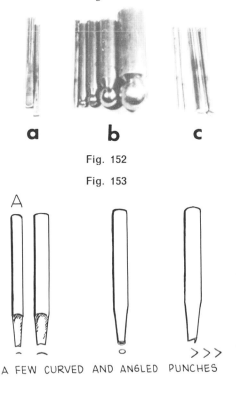

a   b   c

Fig. 152

Fig. 153

A FEW CURVED AND ANGLED PUNCHES

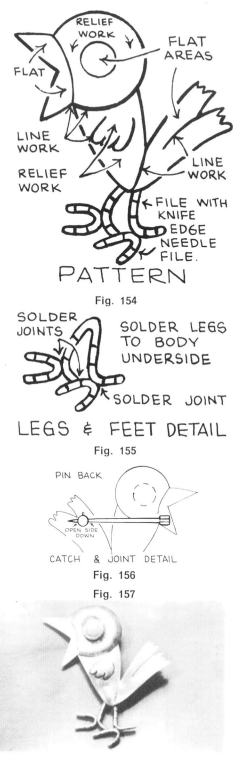

RELIEF WORK

FLAT AREAS

FLAT

LINE WORK

RELIEF WORK

LINE WORK

FILE WITH KNIFE EDGE NEEDLE FILE.

PATTERN

Fig. 154

SOLDER JOINTS

SOLDER LEGS TO BODY UNDERSIDE

SOLDER JOINT

LEGS & FEET DETAIL

Fig. 155

PIN BACK

OPEN SIDE DOWN

CATCH & JOINT DETAIL

Fig. 156

Fig. 157

"LIL BITTY BIRD" PIN (Fig. 157)

Materials

20 gauge sterling sheet for body and tail

12 gauge round wire for legs

1 round cabochon — 9mm

Pin back findings

Project Steps

1. Scribe the pattern (Fig. 154) and line detail, except for the legs, onto the metal sheet.

2. Saw out, then file the edges smooth.

3. Anneal the metal, pickle and rinse.

4. Embed the metal in a pitchbowl, scribed design to the top.

5. Chase lines where indicated. For eye lines, use a small curved punch (Fig. 153A).

6. Turn over the metal and raise in relief the head, body and wing, with the wing and head raised more than the body. Use rounded tools or dapping punches (see *Repousse*, Page 54).

7. Turn over the metal and mount it on wood to flatten the eye area. Use a round, flat-tipped modeling tool and hammer (tool tip edges should be slightly rounded).

8. Repeat steps 6 and 7 until the desired relief is achieved.

9. File and sand away uneven surfaces.

10. Solder the leg and foot detail (Fig. 155) to the body as shown (Fig. 154).

11. Make a bezel collar and solder it to the eye area.

12. Solder a pin joint behind the beak and a catch behind the tail feathers (Fig. 156).

13. With a knife edge needle file, make lines as shown around the top surface of the legs and feet.

14. Apply coloring solution to chased and filed lines and around the eyes (see *Coloring*, Part 9, Pages 34-35). Finish with fine emery cloth — from the eye outward; all in one direction for the rest of the body. Polish the legs and bezel.

15. Mount the stone and pinstem.

Part 15 — Decorative Techniques

Surface Finishes

Texturing metal as a part of the overall design of a piece of jewelry can add greatly to its beauty and interest. A type of texture or surface should be chosen to complement the particular piece. Methods for finishing surfaces are almost limitless. To name only a few texturing processes (Fig. 158): "picked" finish; dented finishes; brushed finish, using emery cloth or paper; file cuts; and textures produced by various tools chucked in a motorized handpiece. A few of the motorized handpiece tools are: brass wire brush (swirls), emery points of different shapes, silicon carbide and emery cutting wheels, and whatever other accessory or method the imagination might conjure up.

PICKED FINISH (Fig. 159) — The metal should at least have a first polishing with tripoli before starting the picked finish. A polished round or square shaped, sharply pointed tool is then used by carefully tapping it with a small hammer to develop a field of small sharp indentations. These are cut in close together at even depths. Done correctly, it produces a sparkling finish that will create reflections like so many tiny diamonds. A carpenter's nail can be fashioned into a temporary "pick."

DENTED FINISHES FROM BLUNT NAILS — This is similar to picked work, but larger and blunter tools are used to stamp in slight indentations. Various sizes of nails make interesting background texture, especially if the work is finished afterwards with a coloring solution, then rubbed with a soft cloth. In Fig. 160, the background was textured with a 20d common nail.

BRUSHED FINISH — to produce a brushed finish, use emery or silicon carbide cloth or paper, from coarse to fine depending on the finish desired. See Part 5, Page 20, for further details.

Fig. 158

Fig. 159

Fig. 160

Fig. 161

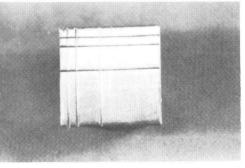

Fig. 162

Fig. 163

DENTED FINISH WITH ROUND TOOLS — This type finish was used in the project for Part 13. A round tipped tool of any size (i.e., dapping punches, steel balls) will produce small overlapping dents by tapping the tool with a small hammer. The ball end of a chasing hammer can also be used. Dented finishes are usually done after the piece has had its first polishing with tripoli.

MOTORIZED HANDPIECE TOOL FINISHES — Experiment with different wheels, points and cutters to learn new and interesting textures. In Fig. 161 the design was ground in with a tiny emery wheel.

FILE CUT DESIGNS — The surface should already be prepared with a first polishing of tripoli, if a polished surface is desired. Start the cuts with a jeweler's saw or by making a line with a graver. Complete by filing the cuts deeper with a knife edge, triangular or square needle file. This method usually works best on flat pieces, such as tops of cigarette cases or pill boxes (Fig. 162).

ENGRAVING — One method of engraving is to use a line graver which cuts several grooves at once. This produces a finish popularly known as florentine. The metal is first secured on an engraving block, a piece of hardwood or a pitchbowl. The graver handle is held firmly in the palm of the hand. The tool is held at enough of an angle to cut shallow grooves into the metal. Controlled forward pressure is applied to the tool so that a continuous series of grooves are made. In one method, the thumb brakes forward movement. Much practice is needed to comfortably use engraving tools.

Line gravers can be used to cut a series of straight lines only (Fig. 163), or with another series of lines crossing at 90° over the first (Fig. 164A), incised slightly lighter than the first. For a different effect (Fig. 164B) the tool can be wiggled back and forth as the cuts are made.

Other engraving tools can be used to cut single lines (Fig. 165) or exquisitely curved designs. Gravers, which come in a variety of widths and styles, are available from jewelry tool suppliers.

Because engraving is an art in itself, the beginning jeweler who wishes to fully learn the technique is advised to study books on the subject and, perhaps, receive personal instruction from a knowledgeable teacher.

APPLIQUE OF SHOT — This is shot which has been soldered to jewelry to form a mound, design or part of a design. These small solid beads of metal give an interesting decorative finish, especially if the piece is treated with coloring solution, such as liver of sulfur, after finishing, and the beads are highlighted by polishing.

PROJECT
BELT BUCKLE WITH APPLIQUE OF SHOT
Materials
18 gauge sheet — top layer
18 or 20 gauge sheet — bottom layer
Scrap silver wire for melting into shot

The pattern (Fig. 166) is to scale and is for a ½-inch wide belt.

Project Steps
1. Scribe the TOP LAYER pattern (Fig. 166A) to the 18 gauge sheet and saw out slightly larger than the outline.

2. Pierce and saw out where shown (Fig. 167 C and D). File smooth to the scribe lines.

3. Sand and polish the pierced area's edges. Clean and rinse.

4. Scribe the BOTTOM LAYER pattern (Fig. 166B) on 18 or 20 gauge sheet and saw out 1/16 inch larger than the outline. Do not file smooth.

5. Flux, then presolder the top of the bottom layer with hard solder, spreading the solder across the top as it melts. Pickle and rinse.

6. Flux, then place the two layers together, presoldered bottom facing the pierced top piece (Fig. 168). Heat the piece with the torch to bring the solder to a molten state, using a large flame (No. 3 tip for Prest-O-Lite torch).

a   **b**

Fig. 164

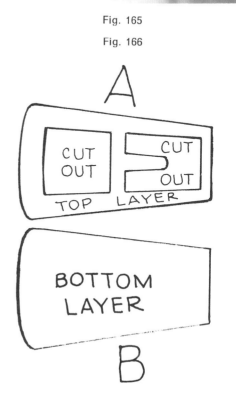

Fig. 165

Fig. 166

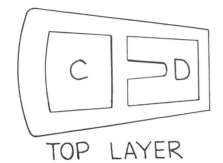

TOP LAYER

Fig. 167

SOLDER TOGETHER

Fig. 168

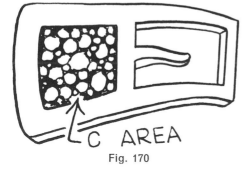

Fig. 169

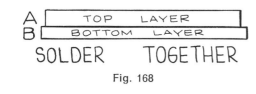

Fig. 170

Fig. 171

Pickle and rinse. Check to see if all seams are solidly soldered. Flux and place solder snippets at any unsoldered seams and heat until they become molten and fill the seams.

7. Pierce area D. Saw out, then file the edges smooth and flush to the top piece.

8. Curve the hook end of the buckle over a mandrel with a rawhide mallet. See the profile of the buckle (Fig. 169) for depth of curve line.

9. Flux, then arrange medium solder snippets around the bottom of recess area C. Then fill with different sized small sterling shot, melted into spheres from scrap bits of wire. Mound them up slightly, filling in open spaces between larger beads with smaller ones (Fig. 170). Flux again. Add tiny snippets of medium solder to all touching points around the beads, and solder them in place. Pickle and rinse. Check for loose shot. Reflux and resolder, if necessary.

10. Curve the hook downward to about a 45° angle. To do this place the buckle over a mandrel and bend the hook with the mallet. Then give the hook tip a slight upward curve with round nose pliers.

11. Saw away excess metal from the bottom layer and file flush to the top piece.

12. Sand, then polish all unfinished surfaces with tripoli. Clean and rinse.

13. Heat the piece to a first sizzle, then drip coloring solution into the beaded area with a small brush. Clean and rinse.

14. Repolish all surfaces (just highlighting the beads) with yellow rouge. Clean and rinse.

15. If desired, finish with red rouge for a mirror-bright polish. Clean and rinse. Figure 171 shows the finished buckle.

NOTE: The book, *Modern Jewelry,* by Graham Hughes, contains many black and white and color plates of jewelry, some with excellent examples of unique surface textures.

Part 16 — Design

Because the study of jewelry design can be rather extensive, this chapter presents only a few of the more important ideas and suggestions which this author feels might be helpful to the beginner. If a piece of jewelry has been designed well, it is esthetically pleasing or exciting to the eye. Whether it is based on natural form, abstraction or freeform is purely a matter of choice.

Experiment

One shouldn't curb the mind into believing that there are only a few cut and dried methods for designing. To do this would soon produce sterile and boring results. Always feel free to try new techniques. Experiment with various combinations of metal forms — wire to sheet, strip curls to sheet, half domes or beads to sheet, etc. (see Fig. 172). Combine brass and copper; or brass, copper and silver in a design; and so on, and so on.

Use paper, dampened cardboard, thin copper sheet, etc., as props for designing. These can be twisted, rolled, bent and contorted into various shapes, lending ideas for forming metal into designs (Fig. 173 — cardboard and paper).

Perhaps you, as a beginning student, are wondering how to actually go about designing your first piece of jewelry. Here are a few ideas for you to consider.

Fig. 172

Fig. 173

Imagination, Curiosity and Intuition

First, the craftsman's knowledge of basic metal construction of jewelry will help him to keep the design practical. His own intuition will usually tell him whether his design is pleasing or not. If a design is successful, it will please

Fig. 174

Fig. 175

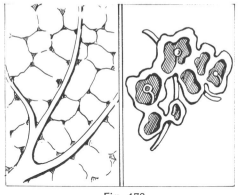
Fig. 176
Fig. 177

others as well as himself, but naturally not everyone. People appreciate art in different ways.

Give your imagination full rein — exercise it; make it work for you. Along with imagination, curiosity ranks high in aiding creativity. Look at the multitude of natural forms about you. See how plants grow; notice the structure of flowers, the graceful curve of long slender stems, the drama of jagged, bare tree limbs.

Become aware of and curious about the interesting things of nature; see how many design ideas can be borrowed from them. There is the Passionflower, for instance, with its layered center. Arranged on top of its petals is a filmy filament resembling a spiked crown, which in turn is topped by five anthers, from which grow three knobby pistils.

Creating designs can be easier than you might imagine. Take a wagon wheel (Fig. 174), for an example. Keep the feeling of the design, but change parts of it — enlarge or lengthen sections, shorten or make others narrow. Balance longer sections against shorter ones. Instead of a monotonous procession of spokes, you now have a varied and more interesting pattern (Fig. 175).

Design from Magnification

Study nature (man-made objects, as well), with a magnifying glass. See how many beautiful sources of design lie so close at hand — in your own back yard, perhaps. Examples of magnification might be: centers of tiny flowers, cellular structure of wood, seed pods, sliced citrus fruit or leaf vein patterns (Fig. 176).

List as many original objects as you can that would make interesting patterns through magnification. View them, then make sketches on 3x5 cards and file by name, alphabetically. Each of these can later become a source or nucleus from which you can create a design.

Doodles and Sketches

Doodle, or sketch, pages of designs from your imagination while ideas are fresh (Fig. 177), then hide them away for a time. Later, when you go back to them, those of merit will immediately stand out from the rest. The design can then be further developed for use as jewelry with a fresh approach.

Tracing paper is an excellent aid for encouraging evolution of designs. Place it over a previous sketch and make improvements while tracing the original.

Balance and Interest

Along with the preceding suggestions, there are a couple of basic mechanical aids which might be helpful to the beginning jewelry designer — balance and interest.

A good way to check for balance is to criticize your own designs, asking: does one side balance pleasingly with the other? Hold it sideways, upside down, right side up, and ask the same question. If the design seems out of balance when turned to any angle, corrections may be in order. A lovely piece of jewelry exhibits a good sense of balance and interest from any viewable position (Fig. 178).

Another way of checking balance is to divide your design in half with a string, vertically, horizontally and at 45° angles (Fig. 179). As much attention should be given to the pleasing shapes and balance of background areas as to design objects (Fig. 180).

While some people appreciate the tranquil simplicity of a symmetrically arranged design, others soon become bored, requiring more variety to excite their imagination. Excitement can be achieved by balancing different sizes and kinds of shapes against each other — line against form, depth against height, dark against light, a large form against small forms of different shapes (Fig. 181). An example of unexciting design interest would be several forms, all the same size and all spaced exactly the same distance apart.

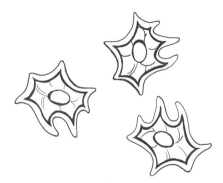

Fig. 178

Fig. 179

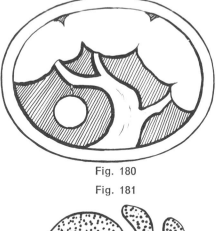

Fig. 180

Fig. 181

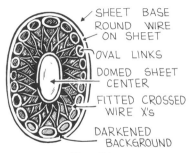

SHEET BASE
ROUND WIRE
ON SHEET
OVAL LINKS
DOMED SHEET
  CENTER
FITTED CROSSED
  WIRE X's
DARKENED
  BACKGROUND

Fig. 182

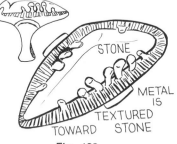

STONE

METAL
IS
TEXTURED
TOWARD STONE

Fig. 183

Added interest can be achieved by incorporating rhythm into the design. What is design rhythm? It is a sensation of activity, leading the eyes across a piece of jewelry with a sense of movement. Figure 182 is an example of how rhythm can be used in a simple symmetrical design. The direction of lines and sense of movement draw the eyes to the center of interest.

A gemstone can often become the center of interest for a piece of jewelry, with the rest of the design complementing it as illustrated in Fig. 183.

Learn to be Original

There is only one way to create beautiful original jewelry, and that is to learn to design your own. How-to articles that you find in rock hobby magazines are very helpful in developing techniques and ideas. Use them, then incorporate what you have learned into your own designs.

A study course in any kind of art design is helpful. Books can be obtained from most libraries. Those of you who lack intuitive artistic creativeness should make an honest effort to use the designing aids about which you have learned. The effort will be rewarding as you experience pride of achievement when you show your original creations.

Figures 184 and 185 show how driftwood and some hors d'oeuvre picks were worked into original designs.

Fig. 184

Fig. 185

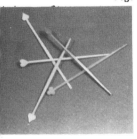

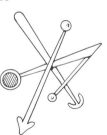

SUPPLEMENTARY SOURCE BOOKS

Rock hobby suppliers, bookstores and libraries have many fine books on jewelry making, a few of which are:

Basic Wax Modeling, *Tsuyuki.* Step by step guide to the design and creation of a wax model, preparing a wax model for casting and the actual casting process. Hard cover, 106 pgs., ISBN 4-905588-28-6.

Gem Tumbling and Baroque Jewelry Making, *Victors.* A guide for amateurs. Includes how to build a tumbler. 58 pgs.

Jewelry: Contemporary Design and Technique, *Evans.* Offers all the information needed to create handmade jewelry and other metal objects. Concise explanations with step-by-step photographs. Hard cover, 296 pgs., ISBN 0-87192-141-3

Jewelry Making Manual, *Wicks.* Clear, easy-to-follow descriptions of basic and advanced techniques, principles of good design, new developments. Black & white and color photos. Hard cover, 174 pgs., ISBN 0-9615984-2-5

Jewelry Repair Manual, *Hardy.* Second edition. Complete guide to techniques of jewelry repair, cleaning and gem setting. 254 pgs. ISBN 0-671-60906-8

Practical Casting, *McCreight.* Excellent textbook about lost wax models, investing, burnout and many other methods and procedures. Clear descriptions of small scale casting. 122 pgs., ISBN 0-9615984-0-9

The Complete Metalsmith, *McCreight.* Tools and techniques for producing metal jewelry. A bestselling workshop manual, abundantly illustrated. 190 pgs., ISBN 0-87192-240-1

Indian Jewelry Making Vol. I and II, *Branson.* All-color presentations of traditional silversmithing methods. Detailed instructions that include designs, tools and techniques. Spiral bound for ease in bench work.
Vol. I-64 pgs., ISBN 0-918080-15-0
Vol. II-64 pgs., ISBN 0-918080-17-7

OTHER GEMBOOKS

JEWELRY MAKING

Jewelry Making for Beginners
Soukup. Here is an easy-to-learn method for fabricating soldered jewelry pieces. All steps are clearly shown with photos and detailed text. Now anyone can learn jewelry crafting with little investment of tools and no previous knowledge or experience.

Jewelry Maker's Handbook
Geisinger. One of the most complete books on jewelry making available. All techniques are shown step-by-step allowing the reader to follow along and create the project in the book, then begin designing and fabricating originals. Profusely illustrated with photos and drawings.

Jewelry Craft Made Easy
French. For the hobbyist and craftsperson who prefers purchasing already finished gemstones, mountings and findings for assembling interesting jewelry. Detailed instructions and profuse illustrations cover a wide variety of men's and women's jewelry.

Handbook of Lost Wax or Investment Castings
Sopcak. A how-to-do manual that shows you how to make the equipment you will need and how to use it to make patterns, molds, and castings for jewelry and small metal parts. Completely illustrated.

How to Design Jewelry
Austin & Geisinger. Design is the element that adds something special to jewelry creations. The questions to design problems are answered here, and much information is given to help you fashion unique jewelry pieces. Illustrated with color and black and white photos, as well as drawings.

MISCELLANEOUS

Handbook of Crystal and Mineral Collecting
Sanborn. You can find no better book to tell you bout minerals and crystals, their physical properties, where and how to collect them, the different types of specimens, how they fit into different types of collections, methods of housing, cataloging, labeling, and much, much more.

The Handbook of Jade
Hemrich. Like no other book on jade ever published. The reader will find just about everything necessary to know in order to find, collect, buy and cut this popular gem material. This is a book for gem cutters, jade collectors, and mineralogists – in fact, for everyone interested in the fact and lore of JADE.

GEM CUTTING

Cabochon Cutting
Cox. Illustrations, photos, and detailed instructions show how to cut a cabochon. Everything to start a craftsperson on the way to expert cutting. Answers all the questions from dopping to setting stones.

Advanced Cabochon Cutting
Cox. Learn how to master special shaped cabochon cutting, assembled stones, star stones, and cat's eyes. Special sections on opal and jade. Sixty-four pages of detailed, illustrated text make this book one of the most useful tools to the gem cutter.

The Art of Gem Cutting
Dake. This is a book that tells how to buy rough stones, cut the gems, choose equipment, and use equipment. It gets the reader started on the right path and builds an interest in the many phases of the hobby of gem cutting. Detailed instructions and complete illustrations.

Handbook of Gemstone Carving
Wertz. An easy-to-follow book on carving gemstones. A complete guide for amateurs with step-by-step instructions for carving flat work, carvings in the round, and portraits in stone. Filled with instructions and photographs.

Facet Cutter's Handbook
Soukup. Here's what the author says: " I took it upon myself to write a book that would help beginners in our club faceting class." This book contains everything one needs to know in order to facet a gemstone expertly. Twenty-two beautiful cuts.

FIELD COLLECTING

Desert Gem Trails
Mary Frances Strong. This is a detailed guide to the gem, mineral, and fossil collecting areas of the Mojave and Colorado deserts of California and adjacent areas in Owens Valley and Nevada. More than 140 localities are mapped out with detailed information. Many illustrations.

Eastern Gem Trails
Oles. A new field guide to gem and mineral localities in the central Atlantic states – New Jersey, Pennsylvania, Maryland, Virginia, and North Carolina – as well as Washington, D.C. All of the famous localities are covered plus many others. The reader can hunt for a host of gem materials, minerals, fossils, and fluorescents.

AVAILABLE FROM YOUR DEALER